Fortress • 43

Roman Legionary Fortresses 27 BC–AD 378

Duncan B Campbell · Illustrated by Brian Delf

Series editors Marcus Cowper and Nikolai Bogdanovic

First published in 2006 by Osprey Publishing
Midland House, West Way, Botley, Oxford OX2 0PH, UK
443 Park Avenue South, New York, NY 10016, USA
E-mail: info@ospreypublishing.com

ISBN 1 84176 895 2

Design: Ken Vail Graphic Design, Cambridge, UK
Cartography: The Map Studio Ltd, Romsey, UK
Index by Alison Worthington
Originated by The Electronic Page Company, Cwmbran, UK
Printed and bound in China through Bookbuilders

06 07 08 09 10   10 9 8 7 6 5 4 3 2 1

A CIP catalogue record for this book is available from the British Library.

FOR A CATALOGUE OF ALL BOOKS PUBLISHED BY OSPREY MILITARY AND AVIATION
PLEASE CONTACT:

NORTH AMERICA
Osprey Direct, C/O Random House Distribution Center, 400 Hahn Road, Westminster,
MD 21157, USA
E-mail: info@ospreydirectusa.com

ALL OTHER REGIONS
Osprey Direct UK, P.O. Box 140, Wellingborough, Northants, NN8 2FA, UK
E-mail: info@ospreydirect.co.uk

www.ospreypublishing.com

Artist's note

Readers may care to note that the original paintings from which
the colour plates in this book were prepared are available for
private sale. All reproduction copyright whatsoever is retained by
the Publishers. All enquiries should be addressed to:

Brian Delf,
7 Burcot Park
Burcot
Abingdon
OX14 3DH
UK

The Publishers regret that they can enter into no correspondence
upon this matter.

Acknowledgements

It is again a pleasure to acknowledge the generosity of colleagues
who provided illustrations for this book, or assisted in their
supply. Although most are acknowledged in the photo captions,
I would like to make particular mention of Prof. Dr Dietwulf Baatz
for permission to use his fortress plans (largely redrawn from von
Petrikovits 1975); Erik Dobat (http: //www.limesfilm.com) for
photographs of Aquincum; René Goguey and Michel Reddé for
photographs of Mirebeau; Dr Johann-Sebastian Kühlborn for
material on the early Augustan fortresses in Germany; Florian
Himmler for photographs of Regensburg; Martin Lemke for
photographs of Novae; Jona Lendering (http: //www.livius.org) for
photographs of Vindobona; Dr Gregory Linton (http:
//www.vkrp.org) for photographs of El-Lejjun; Prof. Dr Mirjana
Sanader for photographs of Tilurium; Dr Jürgen Trumm
(Kantonsarchäologie Aargau, Brugg) for photographs of Vindonissa;
and John Allan (Exeter City Council). Particular thanks are due to
Dr Mike Bishop, who kindly offered a selection of photographs at
very short notice.

The Fortress Study Group (FSG)

The object of the FSG is to advance the education of the public in
the study of all aspects of fortifications and their armaments,
especially works constructed to mount or resist artillery. The FSG
holds an annual conference in September over a long weekend
with visits and evening lectures, an annual tour abroad lasting
about eight days, and an annual Members' Day.
The FSG journal FORT is published annually, and its newsletter
Casemate is published three times a year. Membership is
international. For further details, please contact:

The Secretary, c/o 6 Lanark Place, London W9 1BS, UK

Dedication

To Alan Leslie, celebrating 25 years of friendship and anticipating
the next 25.

A note on the sources

All ancient sources are referenced using the abbreviations
recommended by The Oxford Classical Dictionary. All translations
are my own.

Contents

Introduction

Aerial reconnaissance in the 1980s revealed a 37ha fortress on a hill above the town of Marktbreit (Germany) on the river Main. Ground survey and limited excavation have clarified the polygonal shape of the camp and some of the internal buildings. (© Richard Scharnagel)

The concept of a legionary fortress as a permanent fortification dates from the reign of the emperor Augustus (27 BC–AD 14). In previous centuries, legions had been raised for specific military campaigns and disbanded thereafter. Of course, there was always a need for armies to winter in provinces like Spain, which were too far from Rome for the men to be shuttled backwards and forwards each year. And during protracted campaigns, such as Caesar's conquest of Gaul, it had become usual to quarter the legions in nearby friendly territory, where they were no doubt accommodated in timber huts rather than the leather tents of the campaigning season. But it is only from the time of Augustus that we find a standing army based in permanent quarters in the various provinces of the Roman Empire.

Chronology of the Roman imperial legions

When Augustus reorganized the Roman army following a generation of civil war he decided on 28 legions, which he distributed around the empire. Most were eventually stationed at strategic points for continuing the expansion of Roman power, while maintaining internal security in the frontier provinces. The historian Tacitus, writing around AD 120, briefly records the allocation of legions for the year AD 23, during the reign of Augustus' successor, Tiberius. Following the Varian disaster of AD 9, when three legions were lost in the Teutoburger Forest, the total had fallen to 25: eight legions were on the Rhine (divided between an upper and a lower district), and four were on the Danube, with another two in the Dalmatian hinterland; three lay in Spain, two were in Africa (where one of the Danubian legions was assisting the resident unit to quell a revolt), two were in Egypt and four were in Syria (Tac., *Ann.* 4.5).

We catch another glimpse of the legionary order of battle on a well-known inscription from Rome (ILS 2288), listing the legions in geographical order from west to east (see p. 29). Five legions known to have been raised after AD 165 are tacked onto the end, showing that the list was originally compiled before that date – though not long before, as the legion lost in AD 161 (probably *IX Hispana*) is absent.

From time to time, during the two centuries separating the reigns of Tiberius and Septimius Severus, new legions swelled the numbers under arms. Equally, new units had replaced occasional losses, as individual legions were destroyed in war or, more rarely, disbanded for disgraceful conduct. The historian Cassius Dio, who shared the consulship with the emperor Severus Alexander in AD 229, claimed that only 19 of Augustus' original legions had survived into the 3rd century AD; the other 14 that existed in Dio's day had been raised subsequently (see p. 31ff.). Nor did the legionary bases remain static across the centuries. Major manoeuvres, such as the invasion of Britain in AD 43, or the Dacian Wars of AD 101–2 and 105–6, often entailed the re-assignment of legions and the building of new fortresses. However, by the mid-2nd century AD, the situation had settled down and the legionary bases rarely moved thereafter.

Inscriptions are usually the clearest indicator that a particular legion was present in a given area. However, these can take many different forms. This catapult arrowhead (length, 5.3cm) was found at the Döttenbichl, a religious sanctuary near Oberammergau, and demonstrates the presence of legion *XIX* in the vicinity. (© Author, after W. Czysz et al., *Die Römer in Bayern*, Stuttgart, 1995)

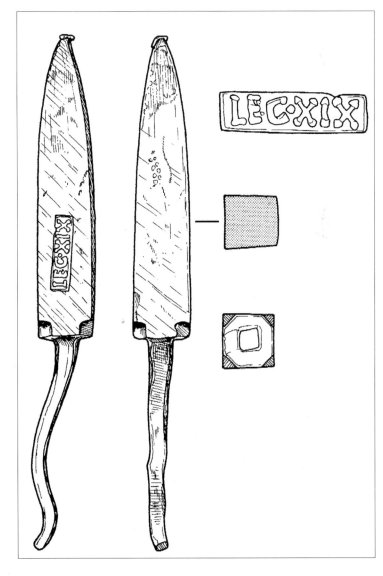

27 BC	Augustus distributes the legions in Gaul (legions *XVI Gallica, XVII, XVIII, XIX, XXI Rapax*), Spain (legions *I, II Augusta, IV Macedonica, V Alaudae, VI Victrix, IX Hispana, X Gemina, XX*), Macedonia (legions *IIII Scythica, V Macedonica, VII, X Fretensis*), Illyricum (probably legions *VIII Augusta, XI, XIII Gemina, XIV Gemina, XV Apollinaris*), Syria (legions *III Gallica, VI Ferrata*), Egypt (legions *III Cyrenaica, XII Fulminata*) and Africa (legion *III Augusta*) (Total: 27 legions)
25 BC	Rome annexes the kingdom of Galatia; the royal troops based there are transferred to Egypt as legion *XXII Deiotariana* (Total: 28 legions)
14 BC	Foundation of the province of Raetia (Switzerland). Legions *XVI Gallica* and *XXI Rapax* perhaps occupy a fortress at Augsburg-Oberhausen; legion *XIX* occupies a fortress at Dangstetten
12–5 BC	Roman armies based at Xanten, Cologne and Mainz (Germany) campaign beyond the Rhine; turf-and-timber fortresses are established along the rivers leading east into Germany (e.g., Haltern, Oberaden, Anreppen on the Lippe; Marktbreit on the Main)
AD 4–5	Campaigns beyond the Rhine briefly resumed
AD 6	Legionary battle group assembled at Carnuntum (Austria) for planned invasion of the kingdom of the Marcomanni (modern Czech Republic); thwarted by revolt in the Pannonian hinterland, lasting for three years
AD 9	Destruction of legions *XVII, XVIII, XIX* in 'Varian disaster' in Germany; widespread troop movements to stop the gap (Total: 25 legions)
AD 30s	Double fortress at Cologne replaced by single bases at Neuss (legion *XX*) and Bonn (legion *I*); legions *V Alaudae* and *XXI Rapax* still at Vetera
AD 39	Emperor Gaius (Caligula) raises legions *XV Primigenia* and *XXII Primigenia* for projected German campaign (Total: 27 legions)
AD 41–54	Reign of Claudius. General rebuilding in stone at many legionary fortresses
AD 43	Invasion of Britain (probably with the four legions later found in garrison); major troop movements elsewhere
AD 46	Annexation of Thrace accompanied by construction of fortress at Novae (Bulgaria)
AD 66	Emperor Nero raises legion *I Italica* for the projected Caspian campaign (Total: 28)
AD 68	Nero raises legion *I Adiutrix* for the civil war; the pretender Galba raises legion *VII Hispana* (or *Galbiana*) in Spain (Total: 30)
AD 69	Emperor Vespasian raises legion *II Adiutrix* (Total: 31)
AD 70	Legions *XV Primigenia* and *V Alaudae* (?) destroyed in civil war; *I Germanica* disbanded in disgrace; *IV Macedonica* and *XVI Gallica* reconstituted as *IV Flavia felix* and *XVI Flavia firma*; *VII Hispana* (or *Galbiana*) becomes *VII Gemina* (Total: 28); Double camp at Vetera replaced by single fortress (Vetera II)
AD 83	Emperor Domitian raises legion *I Minervia* for campaign against the Chatti in Germany (Total: 29)
AD 84/7	Fortress at Inchtuthil (Scotland) founded by legion *II Adiutrix* (?) and rapidly abandoned
AD 89	Domitian officially bans brigading legions together; double fortress at Mainz replaced by single camp
AD 92	Legion *XXI Rapax* (?) destroyed in fighting across the Danube (Total: 28)
C. AD 105	Emperor Trajan raises legions *II Traiana* and *XXX Ulpia* for Second Dacian War (Total: 30)
AD 106	Annexation of Arabia and construction of fortress at Bostra (Syria) by legion *III Cyrenaica*
AD 117	Trajan transfers a second legion to Judaea, probably *II Traiana*, based at Caparcotna (Israel)
AD 122	Legion *XXII Deiotariana* (?) destroyed in rioting in Alexandria (Total: 29)
AD 161	Legion *IX Hispana* (?) destroyed in fighting in Armenia (Total: 28)
AD 165	Emperor Marcus Aurelius raises legions *II Italica* and *III Italica* for Marcomannic War and invasion of Suebian territory (Total: 30)
AD 179	Fortress of Castra Regina (Germany) founded by legion *III Italica*
AD 197	Emperor Septimius Severus raises legions *I Parthica, II Parthica* and *III Parthica* for Parthian expedition; construction of fortress at Albanum (Italy) (Total: 33)
C. AD 200	Fortress at Lauriacum (Austria) founded by legion *II Italica*

The design and development of legionary fortresses

The marching camps of the legions

The Roman army had a long tradition of constructing fortified encampments while on campaign. Simple bank-and-ditch defences enclosed an area criss-crossed by a pattern of streets, dividing the camp into a regular layout that gave the soldiers a familiar reference point in often hostile territory. During the Gallic Wars, although Caesar's legions often wintered amongst allied tribes, they still made sure that their position was fortified properly. And, of course, during siege work, the legions were accommodated in camps. Polybius, writing in the mid-2nd century BC, gives a detailed account of a camp from his own era (Polyb. 6.27–31). The commander's tent, known as the *praetorium*, occupied a central position, flanked by an open assembly area (*forum*) and the tent of the *quaestor*, who was the commander's assistant with particular financial responsibilities; six large tents, one for each of the military tribunes, lay in the same general area. In front and behind, the tents of the ordinary soldiers were laid out in orderly lines, leaving alleys in between.

For the period of the Roman Empire there is the work of Hyginus, entitled *De munitionibus castrorum* ('On fortifying camps'). Although scholars are divided as to the precise dating of this text, placing it anywhere between Domitian and Marcus Aurelius, it is important for the light it sheds on the layout of Roman camps and, by extension, legionary fortresses. It should be emphasized that the analysis is not straightforward, as Hyginus appears to be describing the camp not only of a hypothetical army, but of the most complex army imaginable; besides legionary troops and their auxiliaries, there is a complement of the Praetorian Guard and marines from the imperial fleets, along with various irregular units, including camel-riders. Nevertheless, the principle remains the same. Having selected a suitable location for their camp, the legionary surveyors set up a tool called a *groma*, which allowed them to sight along perpendicular lines. Beginning from the centre of the camp, at the position reserved for the commander's tent (*praetorium*), they laid out a large rectangular area, crossed from side to side by two parallel roads, thus creating

Roman fortresses were often sited near navigable rivers to facilitate the shipment of supplies. During the reign of the Emperor Augustus, the main Roman invasion route into Germania Magna across the Rhine lay along the river Lippe. One of the sites utilized in successive years was Haltern, where the fortress was occupied in the period 5 BC–AD 9. (© Jona Lendering)

three roughly equal slices: the front (*praetentura*), the rear (*retentura*), and the middle, known as the 'flanks of the *praetorium*' (*latera praetorii*). The troops were encamped in blocks in the front and rear and to either side of the *praetorium*.

Legionary fortresses under Augustus (27 BC–AD 14)

In the early years of Augustus' reign, the legions remained mobile strike forces, and were moved around as a matter of course. There was no need for the later practice of hiving off *vexillationes* (detachments) for temporary service elsewhere, when the whole legion could readily move en masse. The final conquest of Spain by 19 BC freed several legions for service elsewhere, and the push to the upper Danube in 16–14 BC brought legions to the area of modern

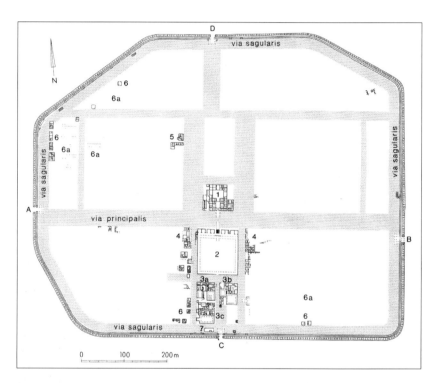

Plan of the 56ha fortress at Oberaden (Germany), which dates from the campaigns of Drusus beyond the Rhine (11–9 BC) and is thus the oldest known fortress. Amongst the numbered buildings are the *praetorium* (1), the *principia* (2), officers' houses (3), centurions' houses (6), and barrack buildings (6a); C marks the *porta praetoria*. (© Westfälische Museum für Archäologie, Münster)

As a general rule, the *praetorium* and *principia* complex lay at the junction of the camp's two main roads. At Marktbreit, the construction trenches of the *principia* show up on the sandy soil as dark lines. (© Dietwulf Baatz)

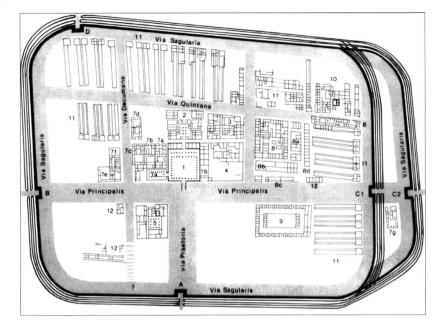

Plan of the 16.7ha (later extended to 18ha) Augustan fortress at Haltern (Germany). Amongst the numbered buildings are the *principia* (1), the *praetorium* (2), officers' houses (7), workshops (8), barrack buildings (11), and a hospital (9). A marks the main gate (*porta praetoria*), and D marks the rear gate (*porta decumana*). (© Westfälische Museum für Archäologie, Münster)

Switzerland, later organized as the province of Raetia. From 12 BC, annual campaigns were launched across the Rhine, resulting in the construction of fortresses on German soil. In AD 6, although Augustus' campaign against the Marcomanni (based in present-day Czech Republic) was abandoned on account of unrest in the Pannonian hinterland, assembling an invasion army of 12 legions must have occasioned large-scale troop movements (Tac., *Ann.* 2.46). Finally, after the Varian disaster of AD 9, the fortresses across the Rhine were given up, and legions were again shuffled around. Thus, for example, legion *XX*, which had departed from Spain in order to participate in the Marcomannic campaign, was briefly quartered at Burnum (Šuplja Crkva, Croatia), before ending up on the lower Rhine in AD 9. The anticipation of further conquest kept arrangements fairly fluid, but excavated fortresses of this date show a remarkable degree of permanence.

In general, the legionary fortresses built on the far side of the Rhine during the reign of Augustus exhibit considerable regularity in their layout, but the terrain heavily influenced the line of their defensive circuit. For example, Marktbreit (near Würzburg, Germany) was strategically located on high ground overlooking the navigable river Main. This last consideration was important for supplying the base by means of water transport, which was cheaper and more convenient than hauling heavy loads along unmetalled roads and tracks. For example, the 40 wooden casks discovered in the fortress at Oberaden (near Dortmund, Germany) were large enough, at 1,200 litres capacity, to present significant transportation difficulties. It was no doubt for this very reason that the fortress was sited on a hill about a mile from the river Lippe, where the terrain forced the Roman surveyors to lay out an irregular, heptagonal circuit. But even at Anreppen (near Paderborn, Germany) in the Lippe valley, the fortress is not a rectangle, as prescribed by Polybius and Hyginus, but an elongated oval.

Despite the generally irregular shape of these early fortresses, the internal layout was strictly based on a grid of rectangular plots. However, where the central focus of the temporary camps described by Polybius and Hyginus was the commander's residence, the *praetorium* in the Augustan fortresses was pushed to the rear of a new central building. This was the *principia*, or headquarters, comprising a square courtyard surrounded by a portico on three sides; on the fourth side, at the rear of the building, lay a single range of rooms flanking a central vestibule, which gave access to the adjoining *praetorium*. These rooms are

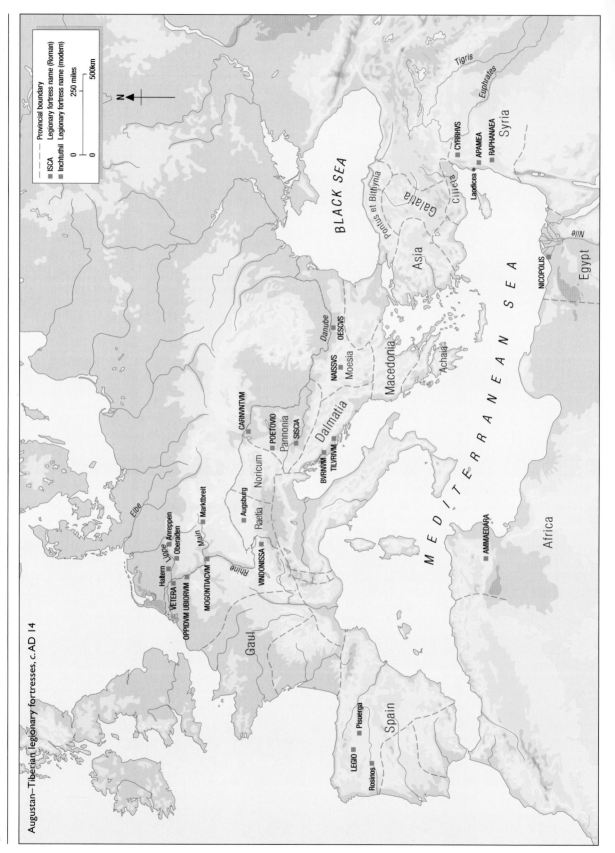

Augustan–Tiberian legionary fortresses, c.AD 14

Legend:
- Provincial boundary
- ISCA — Legionary fortress name (Roman)
- Inchtuthil — Legionary fortress name (modern)

0 — 250 miles
0 — 500km

N

Rivers and regions:
Tigris, Euphrates, Syria, CYRRHVS, APAMEA, RAPHANAEA, Laodicea, Cilicia, Galatia, Asia, Pontus et Bithynia, BLACK SEA, Nile, Egypt, NICOPOLIS, Achaia, Macedonia, Moesia, OESCVS, NAISSVS, Danube, Dalmatia, TILVRIVM, BVRNVM, SISCIA, Pannonia, POETOVIO, CARNVNTVM, Noricum, Augsburg, Raetia, Marktbreit, Main, Elbe, Lippe, Haltern, Anreppen, Oberaden, VETERA, OPPIDVM VBIORVM, MOGONTIACVM, Rhine, VINDONISSA, Gaul, MEDITERRANEAN SEA, Africa, AMMAEDARA, Spain, Pisuerga, LEGIO, Rosinos

Augustan fortress at Marktbreit, c.5 BC

11

A column of troops approaches the north-east gate of the Augustan fortress at Marktbreit (Germany). Its large size (37ha) suggests that two legions were based here, and excavation has indicated a date of c.12 BC–AD 9, although the general dearth of finds points to a relatively short occupation within that period. Following the camp's initial discovery from the air in 1985, further aerial reconnaissance pinpointed two of the gates. On excavation, these were found to be of typical Augustan design, with recessed double portals constructed from massive timbers. Within the camp, the central buildings were revealed by excavation.

The *principia*, with entrance porch projecting onto the north-east to south-west *via principalis*, consisted of the usual open courtyard fronting a double-aisled *basilica* and rear row of rooms incorporating the shrine of the legionary standards. A building lying behind the *principia*, constructed in the style of a Mediterranean peristyle house, is likely to have been the dwelling of one of the legionary commanders. Other buildings in the vicinity no doubt housed the other commander and the legionary tribunes, while the men's barracks must have lain in the unexcavated parts of the camp.

Model of the rear gate (*porta decumana*) of the so-called 'Hauptlager' (main camp) at Haltern (Germany), one of the Augustan camps along the river Lippe. At this early date, fortresses frequently display some irregularity in their internal layout. Here, in order to take advantage of the terrain, the gate is offset some 50m west of the *via decumana* (left side of photo). (© Westfälische Museum für Archäologie, Münster. Photo: S. Brentführer)

Model of a granary (*horreum*) at Anreppen (Germany). Situated around 140km east of the Rhine, the site is the last in a series of fortresses stretching along the river Lippe deep into free Germany. Its isolated position must have required careful provisioning. (© Westfälische Museum für Archäologie, Münster. Photo: S. Brentführer)

thought to have had an administrative function, and thus took over the role of Polybius' *quaestorium*. Equally, the formal access to the commander's residence from the *principia* suggests that the *praetorium* was not simply a grand dwelling, but that certain command functions were carried out there.

In theory, each fortress had four gateways, one per side, creating a crossroads at the *principia*. A visitor entering the fortress by the main gate (*porta praetoria*) would see before him the *principia*'s monumental entrance, down the length of the main street (*via praetoria*). Similarly, anybody exiting the *principia* stepped out onto the main lateral road, called the *via principalis* precisely because it ran past the front of the *principia*; in the distance to his left, he would see the left-hand side gate, known as the *porta principalis sinistra*, and to his right lay the right-hand side gate, known as the *porta principalis dextra*. Only Oberaden, the oldest of the known Augustan fortresses, dating from 11 BC, differs from this scheme. There, the *via principalis* runs between the *principia* and the *praetorium*. But Oberaden demonstrates the general theory that the line of the *via praetoria*, interrupted by the headquarters building and, behind it, the commander's residence, was continued on the far side by the *via decumana*, leading to the *porta decumana* at the rear of the fortress.

Nevertheless, the Augustan surveyors seem occasionally to have taken certain liberties in carrying out their task. Where Hyginus located the

The characteristic foundations of a granary (*horreum*), revealed in the fortress at Anreppen (Germany) during excavations in 2003. The closely spaced trenches held a grid of timber posts supporting a raised floor, so that the circulation of air would keep the granary contents cool and dry. (© Westfälische Museum für Archäologie, Münster. Photo: J.-D. Ludwig)

porta praetoria midway along one of the short sides of his rectangle, there is a marked tendency amongst the Augustan fortresses to define one of the long sides as the front. This can plainly be seen at Haltern (Germany), where the fortress (known as the 'Hauptlager', to differentiate it from other Roman works in the neighbourhood) faces south-east, towards the river Lippe. Similarly, at Marktbreit, the pear-shaped fortress faces north-west, with its long side running parallel to the river valley, 90m below. However, where the *porta praetoria* at Haltern is more or less centrally located on the south-east side, the main gate at Marktbreit is almost at the northern corner. At Oberaden, although the gates are positioned on the four points of the compass, opposites are slightly offset from one another. This is most marked in the case of the *portae principales*, which ought to lie at either end of the *via principalis*; in fact, the east gate deviates to the south, and the west gate to the north, creating a short dog-leg at either end. Similarly, at Haltern, where the side gates are perfectly aligned on the *via principalis*, the *via decumana* has drifted some way to the west of the central axis, and the rear gate (*porta decumana*) even farther, so that it is not even aligned on the *via decumana*.

The extensive use of timber in the construction of these fortresses should not be seen as a temporary measure. It was simply common sense to make use of the most plentiful materials; in the temperate north-west, this meant turf and timber. Whereas Caesar's camps in Gaul had been *hiberna* in the literal sense, occupied through the winter months and abandoned each summer, it is clear that the Augustan fortresses were intended to be permanent bases, from which the legions could operate in enemy territory, secure in the knowledge that their supply lines were safe. And they certainly were well supplied. At Oberaden, besides the casks, whose tell-tale bung-holes imply the import of wine, the analysis of faeces from Roman latrine pits turned up evidence of figs and olives, as well as apples, grapes, sloes and wheat, the soldiers' staple. All of the Augustan fortresses must have been generously equipped with store buildings and granaries; a particularly large example was recently unearthed at Anreppen, and there are suspicions of a grain-drying facility within the ramparts of Marktbreit.

Legionary fortresses under Tiberius (AD 14–37)

On the accession of Tiberius in AD 14, the four legions of the lower German district occupied two double camps, poised for a renewed invasion of Germany beyond the Rhine: Tacitus reports that *I* and *XX* were based at Oppidum Ubiorum (Cologne), while *V Alaudae* and *XXI Rapax* shared a camp at Vetera (Xanten) (Tac., *Ann.* 1.31, 37, 45). In the upper district, *XIV Gemina* and *XVI Gallica* were encamped together at Mogontiacum (Mainz). The other two legions cannot be located with any certainty. Some scholars have placed *II Augusta* near legions *XIV* and *XVI* at Mainz-Weisenau although finds of early

Many areas within the massive 56ha fortress at Vetera remain unexcavated. Archaeology shows that the camp was divided into a western half, occupied by *V Alaudae*, and an eastern half, occupied by *XV Primigenia*. Amongst the numbered buildings are barrack blocks (1 and 2), tribunes' houses (4c and 4d), the two *praetoria* (5a and 5b), and *V Alaudae*'s hospital (10); the shared *principia* (7) lies at the centre. (© Author, after J. E. Bogaers and C. B. Rüger, *Der Niedergermanische Limes*, Köln, 1974)

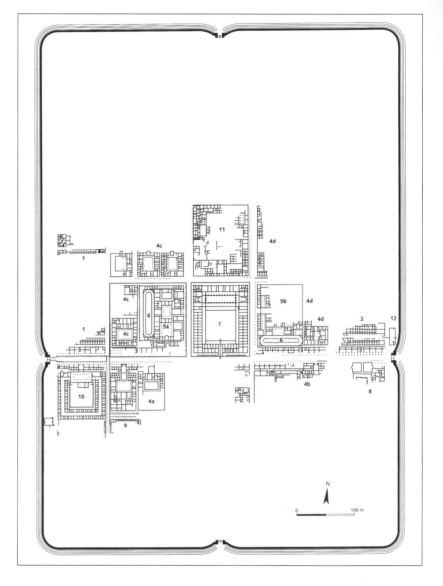

At Burnum (Šuplja Crkva, Croatia), inscriptions attest the rebuilding of the *principia* (headquarters) in AD 50. The remains of the arched façade of the cross-hall (*basilica principiorum*) can still be seen. (© M. C. Bishop)

The rampart of the legionary fortress at Tilurium (Gardun, Croatia), in the Roman province of Dalmatia, exhibits a peculiar series of square socket holes. These are thought to have been connected with a timber framework of some kind. (© M. Sanader)

tombstones from the Strasbourg area suggest the legion's presence there. The fourth legion, *XIII Gemina*, lay to the south, probably at Vindonissa (Windisch, Switzerland), where it could keep a watchful eye on Gaul.

In the same year, according to Tacitus, the three Pannonian legions (*VIII Augusta, IX Hispana, XV Apollinaris*) were brigaded together in a summer camp (Tac., *Ann.* 1.16), though they probably occupied individual *hiberna* at Poetovio (Ptuj, Slovenia), Siscia (Sisak, Croatia) and Carnuntum (Deutsch Altenburg, Austria). In AD 20, *IX Hispana* was temporarily transferred to Africa, for the duration of the war against the Numidian Musulamii (Tac., *Ann.* 3.9; 4.23). At this date, the resident African legion, *III Augusta*, was based at Ammaedara (modern Haïdra in Tunisia), in the Musulamian heartland.

Tacitus reports that two legions garrisoned the lower Danubian province of Moesia (*Ann.* 4.5); these must be *IV Scythica* and *V Macedonica*, which were recorded in AD 33/4 building a towpath along the Iron Gates river gorge. Inscriptional evidence suggests that *V Macedonica* was stationed on the Danube at Oescus (Gigen, Bulgaria), while *IV Scythica* perhaps occupied a rearward base at Naissus (Nis, Serbia). Two legions still occupied the Dalmatian hinterland in present day Croatia, *VII* at Tilurium (Gardun) and *XI* at Burnum (Šuplja Crkva), 'not too distant to be summoned, should Italy suddenly require aid' (Tac., *Ann.* 4.5). Equally, they were presumably stationed there to ensure that the revolt of AD 6 did not flare up again. It is noteworthy that Spain still retained three legions at this time (*IV Macedonica, VI Victrix,* and *X Gemina*), perhaps indicating caution amongst the emperor's advisors: all three seem to have clustered in the north-west and one may even have been based at León, which later became the province's sole fortress.

By now, Augustus' three-legion garrison of Egypt (Strab. 17.1.12), comprising *III Cyrenaica, XXII Deiotariana* and *XII Fulminata*, had been reduced by the transfer of the latter to Syria. Certainly, by 4 BC, the army of Syria numbered three legions (Joseph., *BJ* 2.40), and by AD 19 it had increased to four. At some stage, *X Fretensis* had arrived in the province, where it took up station in the north at Cyrrhus (Kuros, Turkey) (Tac., *Ann.* 2.57). Of the other Syrian legions, *VI Ferrata* lay near Laodicea (Latakia on the Syrian coast) (Tac., *Ann.* 2.79), perhaps at Apamea, but the whereabouts of *III Gallica* remain unknown.

Legionary fortresses under Gaius, Claudius and Nero (AD 37–68)

It is virtually certain that the Emperor Gaius, better known to posterity as Caligula, raised the two legions surnamed *Primigenia*, for his projected German campaign. The numeral of *XV Primigenia* was probably chosen to fit into the sequence of legions already on the upper Rhine (*XIII, XIV* and *XVI*), and it was perhaps initially installed near the latter at Mainz-Weisenau, where the tombstones of four early members have turned up. (It was perhaps at this stage that *II Augusta* lay at Strasbourg.) Gaius' other new legion, *XXII Primigenia*, was probably assigned to a fortress in lower Germany, where the army already included legions *XX* and *XXI*. At some point in the AD 30s, the double fortress at Cologne had been given up and its two legions, *I* and *XX*, installed in separate bases, namely Bonna (Bonn) and Novaesium (Neuss). But *V Alaudae*

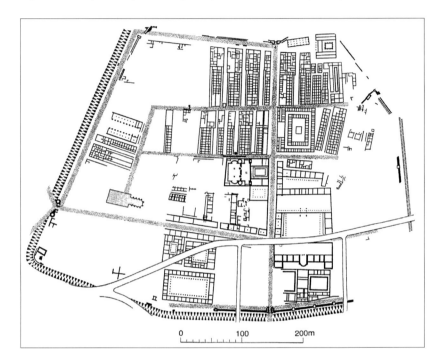

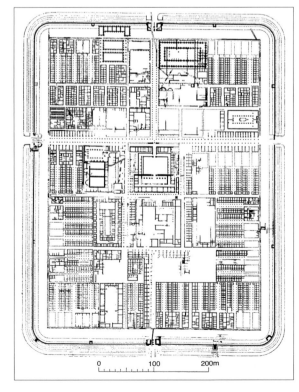

and *XXI Rapax* still lay at Vetera, and it is not clear where the new legion could have fitted in. At any rate, during Gaius' short reign, the army on the Rhine must have stood at ten legions. However, Claudius soon drew off three of these (*II Augusta*, *XIV Gemina*, *XX*) for his invasion of Britain in AD 43, accompanying *IX Hispana* from Pannonia. And some years later, action on the lower Danube with the annexation of Thrace (modern Bulgaria) entailed further legionary movements.

The departure of *IX Hispana* for Britain left Pannonia with only two legions and a vacant fortress at Siscia, but the withdrawal of three Rhine legions initiated a major reshuffle. First, *XVI Gallica* was moved from the upper Rhine fortress of Mogontiacum to the lower Rhine fortress of Novaesium, taking the place of legion *XX*. The simultaneous transfer of *XXII Primigenia* from the lower Rhine to Mogontiacum essentially cancelled out this move. The departure of *XIV Gemina*, which had shared the Mogontiacum fortress, was offset by the arrival of a Spanish legion, *IV Macedonica*; it has left evidence of its presence in the right half of the double fortress, while the left half now accommodated *XXII Primigenia*, each legion keeping itself to one side or the other. Finally, the departure of *II Augusta* returned both armies to a strength of four legions. A second round of moves was initiated by the transfer of *VIII Augusta* to a new fortress at Novae (Steklen, Bulgaria), increasing the army of Moesia to three legions; its place at Poetovio was taken by *XIII Gemina*, moving east from Vindonissa, which itself became the home of *XXI Rapax*. It was probably at this stage that *XV Primigenia* arrived in the lower district to take the latter's place at Vetera; tile-stamps show that the right half of the fortress remained the preserve of *V Alaudae*, while *XV Primigenia* occupied the area to the left. These moves finally reduced the upper Rhine army to three legions.

Early in Nero's reign, with trouble threatening in the East, a western legion was moved to Syria; Tacitus records that it came 'from Germany' (Tac., *Ann.* 13.35), but the legion in question was, in fact, *IV Scythica*, which (as far as we know) never served on the Rhine (cf. *Ann.* 15.6). Its place in Moesia seems to have been filled by legion *VII* (which, along with *XI*, had been named *Claudia pia fidelis* for loyalty to Claudius during an attempted coup in AD 42); at around this time, it vacated its Tilurium fortress and built a new base at Viminacium (Kostolac/Pozarevac in modern Serbia), in the process reducing the garrison of Dalmatia to one legion. Some years later, in AD 62, an escalation of hostilities in the east required the release of two Syrian legions, *IV Scythica* and *XII Fulminata* (Tac., *Ann.* 15.6), for service further north in Cappadocia; and in the following year, the Syrian army was again reinforced by the transfer of another two units from the Danube front, *V Macedonica* (Tac., *Ann.* 15.9) and *XV Apollinaris* (Tac., *Ann.* 15.25). The former was not replaced at Oescus, thus reducing the Moesian army to two legions again, but *X Gemina* was withdrawn from Spain to ensure that the key fortress at Carnuntum remained occupied. Meanwhile, having disgraced themselves in action, the two legions of Cappadocia were returned to Syria, and a fresh army, comprising the two new arrivals alongside *III Gallica* and *VI Ferrata*, was mustered at Melitene (Malatya in eastern Turkey) for an invasion of Armenia (Tac., *Ann.* 15.26). Thereafter, *XV Apollinaris* was briefly despatched to

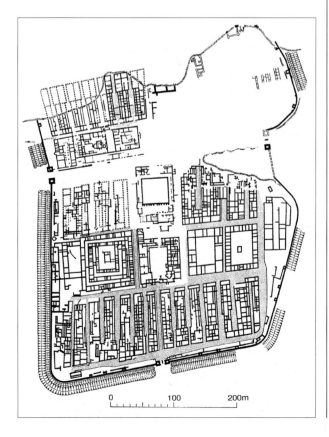

Plan of the legionary fortress at Carnuntum (Bad Deutsch-Altenburg, Austria), which sits on a terrace above the Danube in the Roman province of Pannonia. Excavations carried out in the 19th and early 20th centuries did not distinguish between the various periods of rebuilding, and most of the structures shown on the plan probably date from the 3rd century, when *XIV Gemina* was in garrison. (© Dietwulf Baatz)

0   100   200m

In the aftermath of a civil war that had seen four emperors in rapid succession, a renegade Roman auxiliary officer (Julius Civilis) and his Batavian auxiliaries enlisted the aid of German barbarians to attack the legionary fortress at Vetera on the Rhine. The historian Tacitus describes how the barbarians attempted to demolish the ramparts by piling up firewood, but this proved their undoing when night fell, for the firelight made them clearly visible to the legionaries, who were able to pick them off one by one.

Meanwhile, the Batavian auxiliaries, trained in the warfare of the Romans, built a two-storey tower and moved it up to the gates, where the approach was smoothest. But the besieged legionaries were able to break it apart with stout poles and wooden beams. Furthermore, the legionaries' engineering skills enabled them to construct their own machinery, such as the crane, with which they snatched up individual attackers and tossed them into the camp to be finished off.

Each legion manufactured its own roofing tiles, which were commonly stamped with the unit's name. This tile, from the fort of Saalburg (Germany), carries the capricorn symbol of *XXII Primigenia*, and shows that the legion was involved in construction work there.
(© Jona Lendering)

Egypt (Joseph., *BJ* 3.8). The various winter bases of the other eastern legions remain elusive, but it has been suggested that *XII Fulminata* already lay at its future base of Raphanaea (Rafniye in present day Syria), as it was chosen in AD 66 to spearhead an expedition across the border to Jerusalem (Joseph., *BJ* 7.18).

At the other end of the empire, having secured Colchester as the capital of the new province of Britannia, the four legions fanned out to crush any resistance in southern England. Legion *II Augusta*, commanded by the future emperor Vespasian, marched west, finally establishing a fortress at Exeter around AD 55. Meanwhile, *IX Hispana* marched due north to Lincoln, while *XIV Gemina* and *XX* (shortly to become *XX Valeria Victrix*) probably constructed fortresses in the north-west at Wroxeter and Usk.

Late in his reign, Nero planned a punitive expedition to the Caspian Gates (Dio 62.8.1); he raised a new legion, *I Italica*, for the purpose (Suet., *Nero* 19.2), and *XIV Gemina* was ordered to make its way across the empire from its base in Britain. But events were overtaken by the outbreak of war in the minor province of Judaea, the so-called First Jewish War, which was to occupy three legions (*V Macedonica* and *X Fretensis* from Syria, *XV Apollinaris* from Egypt) until AD 70. Meanwhile, the death of Nero plunged the Roman world into 18 months of civil war. First, Galba, the elderly governor of Tarraconensis (northern Spain), declared himself emperor; with only one legion at his disposal, *VI Victrix*, he promptly raised another, which he numbered *VII*. (At *Hist.* 2.86, Tacitus calls it *VII Galbiana*, but inscriptions suggest that it was officially styled *VII Hispana*.) On Galba's arrival at Rome, he received another legion, *I Adiutrix*, which Nero had begun recruiting from the marines of the Italian fleets (Dio 55.24.2). It is not clear where these new units found accommodation, and we can well imagine that 'the city was crowded with an unusual army' (Tac., *Hist.* 1.6). Simultaneously, the commander on the lower Rhine, Vitellius, was persuaded to make a bid for empire, and found that his opponent was now Galba's erstwhile colleague, Otho, who had ousted the old man early in AD 69. But after defeating Otho's forces at Bedriacum in the north of Italy, Vitellius was in turn defeated by Flavian forces loyal to Vespasian, the commander in Judaea.

Legionary fortresses under the Flavians: Vespasian and Titus (AD 70–81)

The upheavals of civil war had sent legions far from their homes. For example, in AD 69, *III Gallica* made its way west through Moesia, destroyed a band of Sarmatian Roxolani who were troubling the province (Tac., *Hist.* 1.79) and participated in the battle of Bedriacum, where its predominantly eastern recruits famously saluted the rising sun; the legion subsequently returned to Syria (*Hist.* 4.39). Similarly, *XIV Gemina*, having reached north Italy, was turned around and sent back to Britain (Tac., *Hist.* 2.66). Under these circumstances,

The defence of the fortress at Vetera (Xanten), AD 69

North gate (*porta decumana*) of the fortress at Mirebeau (near Dijon, France), flanked by two enormous projecting horseshoe-shaped towers, 9m long by 6m wide. (© Archéologie aérienne René Goguey)

Although the fortress at Satala (Sadak in Turkey) has never been excavated, the familiar playing-card shape of the classic legionary fortress remains visible in the present landscape. The fortress commanded the strategic routes east, from Cappadocia to Persia, and south, from the Black Sea region to Syria. (© D. Kennedy)

legions were either billeted on nearby towns or accommodated in temporary camps. The situation was further complicated by the revolt of the Batavian auxiliaries under their commander Julius Civilis late in AD 69, which caused chaos amongst the Rhine garrisons. Three legions (*I Germanica*, *IV Macedonica*, and *XVI Gallica*) compromised themselves by going over to the rebels. Meanwhile, in the absence of its sister legion *V Alaudae*, *XV Primigenia* was destroyed at Vetera after having endured a siege of several months (*Hist.* 4.22–23, 28–30, 60). Only Vindonissa and its garrison, *XXI Rapax*, escaped the upheavals (*Hist.* 4.61).

With the cessation of hostilities, the new emperor, Vespasian, took stock of the legionary establishment, making changes wherever necessary. In particular, the remnants of *I Germanica* were probably merged with Galba's legion *VII* to make *VII Gemina* (the title *Gemina* is known to have indicated the merging of two units to make a new one), while the mutinous legions *IV Macedonica* and *XVI Gallica* were disbanded and reconstituted as *IV Flavia felix* and *XVI Flavia firma* (taking Vespasian's family name). Understandably, the Rhine garrisons were completely reorganized. In the lower district of Germania Inferior, the Bonna fortress now received *XXI Rapax* as its garrison, and *X Gemina* built a new fortress at Noviomagus (Nijmegen, Netherlands) to watch the territory of the Batavians. Other new fortresses were built at Vetera by *XXII Primigenia* (replacing the old two-legion base there), and at Novaesium by *VI Victrix* (finally ending its century-long association with Spain). In the upper district of Germania Superior, *I Adiutrix* (briefly in Spain under Vitellius) and *XIV Gemina* (which had shuttled backwards and forwards from Britain) were posted to Mogontiacum, while *XI Claudia* (lately at Burnum) was assigned to Vindonissa; *VIII Augusta* (which had founded the fortress at Novae) now constructed a new fortress at Mirebeau (near Dijon, France).

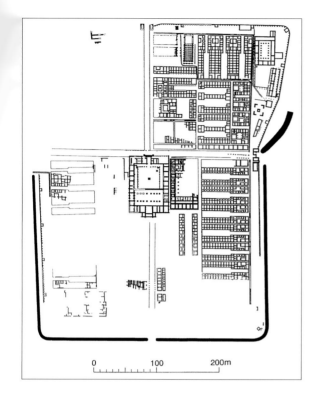

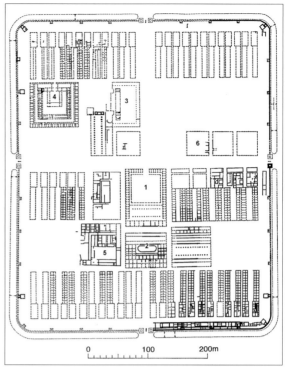

These changes had obvious repercussions elsewhere. In a few cases, new legions were on hand to fill the gaps. In Britain, the arrival of *II Adiutrix* made up for the loss of *XIV Gemina*; the new legion was perhaps posted to Lindum (Lincoln), where it has left inscriptional evidence. At around the same time, the other three legions constructed new fortresses, *II Augusta* at Isca (Caerleon), *IX Hispana* at Eburacum (York), and *XX Valeria Victrix* at Deva (Chester). In Dalmatia, the fortress at Burnum, vacated by *XI Claudia*, became the home of *IV Flavia*. In Moesia, while Viminacium remained the headquarters of *VII Claudia*, the place of *VIII Augusta* at Novae was taken by *I Italica*, which was destined to remain in garrison there for the remainder of its history. Also in that province *V Macedonica* returned from a ten-year tour of duty in the east and refurbished the fortress at Oescus. Some scholars believe that *V Alaudae* formed part of the Moesian army at this time; the tombstone of a serving soldier, found at Scupi (Skopje, Macedonia), has been taken to indicate the legion's presence there, but is seems unlikely that it survived the events of AD 70. Meanwhile in Pannonia, the fortress at Carnuntum, vacated by *X Gemina*, once again became the home of *XV Apollinaris*, returning (like *V Macedonica*) from the Jewish War; it has left evidence of rebuilding there at this time. And the fortress at Poetovio continued to be occupied by *XIII Gemina*.

In the East, the legionary fortresses have always proved elusive, partly because of the tradition of billeting troops on towns there (e.g., Tac., *Ann.* 13.35). According to the Hadrianic writer Suetonius, Cappadocia was upgraded to 'consular' status, with the appointing of an ex-consul as governor (Suet., *Vesp.* 8.4); such senior status implies that more than one legion garrisoned the province. Certainly, the doubly disgraced *XII Fulminata* now lay on the upper Euphrates at Melitene (Malatya, Turkey) (Joseph., *BJ* 7.18), but *XVI Flavia* does not appear to have arrived at Satala (Sadak, Turkey) until AD 76, for it is found in the previous year contributing to a work detail in Syria (AE 1983, 927). Of the other three Syrian legions, *IV Scythica* has left tile stamp evidence in the vicinity of Zeugma (Belkis, Turkey), an important crossing point on the upper Euphrates, although no trace of a fortress has survived. Similarly, although no

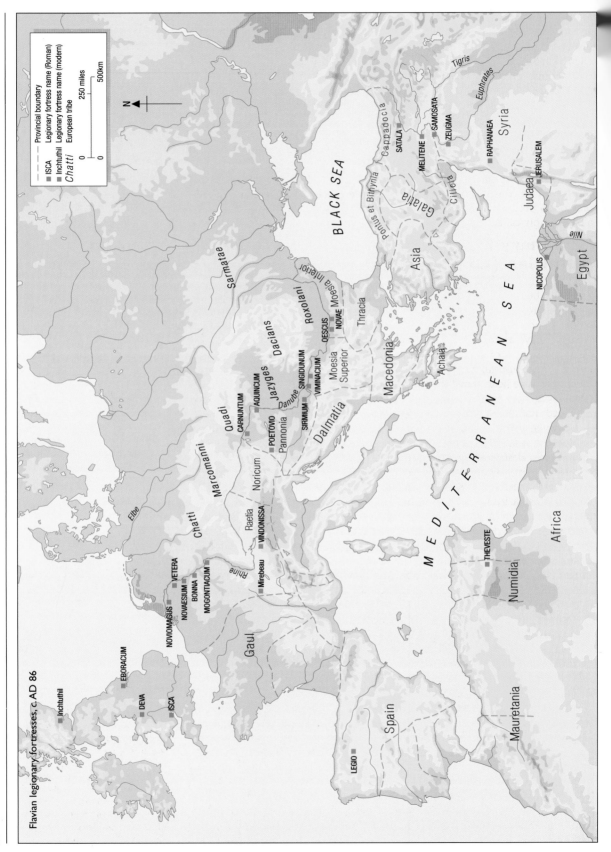

Flavian legionary fortresses, c. AD 86

Inchtuthil
ISCA — Legionary fortress name (Roman)
Inchtuthil — Legionary fortress name (modern)
Chatti — European tribe
— — — Provincial boundary

N

0   250 miles
0   500km

Inchtuthil

EBORACUM

DEVA

ISCA

NOVIOMAGUS
VETERA
NOVAESIUM
BONNA
MOGONTIACUM

Mirebeau

VINDONISSA

Gaul

Rhine

Raetia

Noricum

Chatti

Elbe

Marcomanni

Quadi
CARNUNTUM
POETOVIO
Pannonia

AQUINCUM
Danube
SINGIDUNUM
SIRMIUM
VIMINACIUM
Jazyges

Dalmatia

Dacians

Roxolani

OESCUS
NOVAE
Moesia Inferior

Moesia
Superior

Thracia

Macedonia

Achaia

Sarmatae

BLACK SEA

Pontus et Bithynia

Galatia

Cappadocia

SATALA

MELITENE

SAMOSATA

ZEUGMA

Asia

Cilicia

Syria

RAPHANAEA

JERUSALEM

Judaea

Tigris

Euphrates

Nile

NICOPOLIS

Egypt

MEDITERRANEAN SEA

LEGIO

Spain

Mauretania

Numidia

THEVESTE

Africa

22

fortress has been discovered at Raphanaea, *VI Ferrata* erected inscriptions there at around this time (e.g., CIL 13, 14165). In AD 72, the same legion was responsible for capturing Samosata (Samsat, Turkey), the capital of the tiny client kingdom of Commagene (Joseph., *BJ* 7.224–5), but it seems that *III Gallica* established a base there (ILS 8903). Finally, although *V Macedonica* and *XV Apollinaris* returned to Europe, *X Fretensis* remained in Judaea (Joseph., *BJ* 7.5, 17). Consequently, it was now upgraded to a one-legion 'praetorian' province, where the legionary commander (an ex-praetor who had not yet held the consulship) doubled as the governor.

In Egypt, the double camp at Nicopolis, near Alexandria, remained the base of *III Cyrenaica* and *XXII Deiotariana* throughout the time of the Flavians, while along the coast in north Africa, the resident legion, *III Augusta*, marched 35km south-west to construct a fortress at Theveste (Tébessa, Algeria) in the new praetorian province of Numidia. The single Spanish legion, *VII Gemina*, lay at a base simply called Legio (León).

Legionary fortresses under the Flavians: Domitian (AD 81–96)

The historian Tacitus generally rated Vespasian and his older son Titus highly as emperors, but had a distinctly jaded picture of the younger son. 'Setbacks in the west', he wrote (*Hist.* 1.2), summarizing Domitian's reign. In AD 83, the emperor prepared for war against the Chatti, and even travelled to the Rhine himself. He seems to have assembled a large force at Mirebeau. Roofing tiles found there carry the stamps of five different legions: the four Upper German legions (*I Adiutrix, VIII Augusta, XI Claudia, XIV Gemina*), along with *XXI Rapax*, which must now have been transferred from the lower Rhine; its place at Bonna was taken by a new legion, *I Minervia*. (The enrolling of new legions normally indicated that the annexation of territory was envisaged.)

However, trouble was already brewing on the Danube, where the governor of Moesia was killed in battle against the Dacians. (Some scholars claim that *V Alaudae* was destroyed in this conflict, but the legion had probably already ceased to exist.) The situation remained stable until AD 86, when another Roman army met with disaster in Dacia (present-day Romania). Domitian now divided Moesia into a lower province (Moesia Inferior) to the east, and an upper province (Moesia Superior) to the west, creating two separate legionary commands. The fortresses at Novae (*I Italica*) and Oescus (*V Macedonica*) now belonged to the lower province. Meanwhile, in Upper Moesia, facing the heartland of the Dacians, the existing fortress at Viminacium was supplemented by a new foundation at Singidunum (Belgrade, Serbia); the

The site of Novae (Steklen, Bulgaria), viewed from the north-west, with the defences picked out in red; the Danube lies to the left of the photograph. The main east–west road, showing as a light-coloured band, is slightly offset from the line of the *via principalis*. The distinctive plan of the hospital (*valetudinarium*) can be seen against the north rampart. (© Antiquity of Southeastern Europe Research Center, Warsaw University)

The *porta praetoria* at Aquincum (Budapest, Hungary) lay on the eastern side of the fortress, overlooking the Danube. Remains dating from the 3rd century AD have been consolidated and laid out for visitors. (© Erik Dobat)

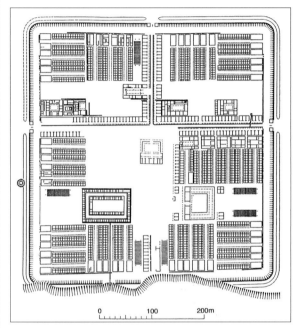

Plan of the legionary fortress at Inchtuthil, situated on high ground above the river Tay in Perthshire (Scotland). Fourteen seasons of selective excavation revealed the layout of the entire timber-built fortress, abandoned while still under construction in *c*. AD 87. Its Roman name remains unknown, but may well have been Victoria. (© Dietwulf Baatz)

arrival of *IV Flavia* as its garrison finally deprived Dalmatia of a legionary army.

Pannonia, too, was strengthened, with the transfer of *II Adiutrix* from Britain. Campaigning had proceeded apace there, and construction of a new fortress was under way, well to the north at Inchtuthil (Scotland). Its intended garrison is not known, but may well have been *II Adiutrix*. Equally, the fortress's Roman name is unknown, but the Hadrianic geographer Claudius Ptolemy, drawing upon Flavian sources, mentions a place called Victoria in eastern Scotland, which might be the fortress. Others prefer the placename Pinnata castra ('winged camp'), claiming that it somehow refers to Inchtuthil's masonry ramparts, a novelty in Scotland at this time. At any rate, the reduction of the provincial army to three legions necessitated considerable retrenchment, so the fortress was vacated and demolished. When *II Adiutrix* arrived in Pannonia, work began on a new fortress at Aquincum (Budapest, Hungary), on the Danube bend.

Further upheaval ensued in AD 89, when the commander on the Upper Rhine, L. Antonius Saturninus, seized the savings of the two Mogontiacum legions to fund a rebellion (Suet., *Dom.* 7.3). Order was quickly restored by his Lower Rhine counterpart, A. Lappius Maximus, whose legions – *I Minervia* at Bonna, *VI Victrix* at Novaesium, *X Gemina* at Noviomagus and *XXII Primigenia* at Vetera – all received the additional honorary titles of *pia fidelis* ('loyal and faithful') from the grateful emperor. Even *VII Gemina* was mobilized by its legate, the future emperor Trajan, to march from Spain in support of the emperor.

But the crisis had three important repercussions. First, two legions would never again be allowed to share a fortress, except in the anomalous case of Egypt, where no senators were allowed and the army was administered by equestrians, who lacked the necessary seniority to foment rebellion. Second, the two military districts on the Rhine were regularized as consular provinces: in the north, Lower Germany (Germania Inferior), and in the south, Upper Germany (Germania Superior). And third, although *VIII Augusta* at Mirebeau and *XI Claudia* at Vindonissa were distant from the rebellion, the other three legions had perhaps been implicated in the affair and were consequently reshuffled. It is widely believed that *XXI Rapax* was now transferred to the Danube front, but its new fortress has never been identified. Similarly, *I Adiutrix* and *XIV Gemina* can no longer have shared the Mogontiacum fortress, which would have violated Domitian's new one-legion regulation. *I Adiutrix* perhaps departed now for the Danube, and may well have occupied the fortress that has been suspected in the neighbourhood of Sirmium (Sremska Mitrovica, Serbia).

The Saturninus affair was not to be the last of Domitian's troubles. During a second strike against the Chatti, who had been implicated in the rebellion, war on the Danube again threatened, and was only averted by diplomacy: Domitian gave the Dacians men and money (Dio 67.7), but the eastward trickle of legions perhaps suggests that this was seen to be a short-term solution. Certainly, only a few years later, he was obliged to mount an *expeditio Suebica et Sarmatica* ('expedition against the Suebians and Sarmatians'; ILS 1017). Suebian tribes called the Marcomanni and the Quadi occupied territory across the Danube from Pannonia in the present-day Czech Republic and Slovakia; their eastern neighbour on the Hungarian plain, again facing Pannonia, was the Sarmatian tribe of the Jazyges, whose kinsmen, the Roxolani, lived further downriver, separated from them by the mountainous land of the Dacians. The Roxolani had given trouble in AD 69, when *III Gallica* was on hand to repulse them (see p. 18), but the new threat posed by the Marcomanni and Quadi was destined to rumble on for decades.

In AD 92, Domitian personally supervised campaigning on the Danube, but his forces suffered a reverse during which the Sarmatians destroyed a legion (Eutrop. 7.23.4), thought to be *XXI Rapax*. Many scholars believe that *XIV Gemina*, which has left evidence of its presence at Ad Flexum (Ungarisch Altenburg, Hungary), was brought from Mogontiacum as its replacement now, although some would delay the transfer until around AD 100. (At any rate, the key fortress at Mogontiacum became the base of *XXII Primigenia*, which must now have vacated Vetera.) By the time of Domitian's death, the Danube armies stood at an unprecedented eight (perhaps even nine) legions, with at least four in Pannonia (*I Adiutrix* perhaps at Sirmium, *II Adiutrix* at Aquincum, *XIII Gemina* at Poetovio, and *XV Apollinaris* at Carnuntum), two in Upper Moesia (*IV Flavia* at Singidunum and *VII Claudia* at Viminacium), and two in Lower Moesia (*I Italica* at Novae and *V Macedonica* at Oescus).

Legionary fortresses under Trajan (AD 98–117)

Warfare on the Danube appears to have continued during the short reign of the elderly Nerva (AD 96–98), to judge from reports of a *bellum Suebicum* ('war with the Suebi'; ILS 2720). Matters were soon taken in hand by Nerva's successor, the emperor Trajan, hailed by posterity as both *optimus* ('best') and *fortissimus* ('bravest'). He is probably responsible for moving two legions up to the river frontier from bases in the hinterland: *I Adiutrix* made the long trek from Sirmium up beyond the Danube bend, where it began construction of a fortress at Brigetio (Szöny, Hungary); likewise, *XIII Gemina* vacated its base at Poetovio for a new frontier fortress at Vindobona (Vienna, Austria). Finally, in AD 101, having strengthened the Suebic sector, Trajan was ready to launch an invasion of Dacia. The following years saw a major upheaval in the distribution of the legions.

The west ditch of the fortress of Vindobona (Vienna, Austria) today survives in the road known as the 'Tiefe Graben' (deep ditch). The road which crosses over on the bridge ('Hohe Brücke') follows the line of the *via principalis*. (© Jona Lendering)

By and large, emperors avoided depleting provincial armies by withdrawing entire legions for service elsewhere. In the AD 20s, *IX Hispana* had been absent from Pannonia for three years serving in Africa (see p. 15), but it became more usual to draw off detachments, the so-called vexillations, for combat and other duties. For this First Dacian War (AD 101–2), besides the legions already on the Danube, Trajan drew vexillations from the eastern legions, and called upon the entire *I Minervia* from Bonna (CIL 2, 2424), *X Gemina* from Noviomagus (AE 1965, 121), and *XI Claudia* from Vindonissa (AE 1934, 177). While its ram emblem has identified the first of these in the thick of the action on Trajan's Column, the others remained behind the lines, releasing *I Adiutrix* and *II Adiutrix* from their respective bases for active service. Late in AD 102, after enduring two summers of fighting, Decebalus, the Dacian king, sued for peace; he was expelled from his capital at Sarmizegetusa (Hatseg, Romania), and a legionary fortress was constructed by *IV Flavia* nearby.

In the years leading up to AD 105, Decebalus perhaps showed signs of breaking the peace, for Trajan now raised two legions, *II Traiana* and *XXX Ulpia*, a sure sign that he intended to occupy new territory. Scholars disagree about precisely when the legions were raised, and in what order. Most agree that the selection of the number XXX implies that there were 29 others in existence. But Trajan inherited only 28. Consequently, some have taken the extreme view that either *V Alaudae* or *XXI Rapax* must have survived beyond AD 100. Of course, the obvious solution is to accept that *II Traiana* was Rome's 29th legion, and *XXX Ulpia* her 30th. The great legionary scholar Emil Ritterling realized this, but believed that *II Traiana* had been so numbered to reflect honour on one of the *legiones primae*, the legions numbered I. This eccentric theory was rightly criticised by the classicist Henry Parker, who preferred to believe that *II Traiana* was numbered thus as Trajan's second creation; in order to keep the arithmetic correct, he created a convoluted scenario whereby *XXI Rapax* survived until *XXX Ulpia* was mobilized, but then disappeared in mysterious circumstances, requiring Trajan to raise a second legion. However, it seems most logical to suggest that Trajan first created *II Traiana*, either in continuance of the numerical sequence begun by *I Minervia* (the last new creation), or as a companion to one of the *legiones primae*, just as Gaius had raised *XXII Primigenia* to serve alongside *XXI Rapax* (see p. 15); the most obvious candidate is *I Italica*, and it is reasonable to suggest that the new legion was initially posted to Moesia Inferior. (In fact, one inscription suggests that *I Italica* and *II Traiana* were under a joint command at some point; ILS 1038.)

The Second Dacian War (AD 105–6) resulted in the creation of a new consular province across the Danube. Sarmizigetusa continued to be occupied by *IV Flavia*, while *XIII Gemina* constructed a fortress at Apulum (Alba Julia, Romania), apparently assisted by *I Adiutrix*, which may have remained in Dacia for several years. At the same time, Trajan had probably realized the vulnerability of the lower Danube frontier, which was virtually ungarrisoned downstream from Novae. As *XI Claudia* would no longer be needed at Brigetio, with the return of *I Adiutrix* from campaigning in Dacia, it must have seemed wise for that legion to construct a new fortress at Durostorum (Silistra, Bulgaria), 150km east of *I Italica* at Novae. Also, either now or a few years earlier, *V Macedonica* vacated its fortress at Oescus and marched 400km downstream to construct a new base at Troesmis (Iglita, in the Dobruja region of Romania). Thus, Lower Moesia acquired a garrison of three legions (or even four, if *II Traiana* was based there), with fortresses evenly spaced along the frontier. By contrast, Upper Moesia retained only one legion, *VII Claudia* at Viminacium, as the fortress of Singidunum had been vacated in order to provide a garrison for Dacia.

Following the example of Moesia, Pannonia was now divided into two. Lower Pannonia (Pannonia Inferior), with Aquincum as its only fortress, had praetorian status, so the first governor, the future Emperor Hadrian, was also commander of the legion (*II Adiutrix*). The whereabouts of Aquincum's previous occupants, *X Gemina*, are unknown, although a fortress has been suspected at Mursa (Osijek in present-day Croatia). Upper Pannonia (Pannonia Superior) was organized as a consular province, with the new foundations at Brigetio and Vindobona joining the long-established fortress of *XV Apollinaris* at Carnuntum. On the transfer of *XIII Gemina* to Dacia, *XIV Gemina* moved into the fortress at Vindobona to complete its construction. Meanwhile, the gradual depletion of the Rhine armies to reinforce the Danube had left only two legions in each of the German provinces. On the upper Rhine, *VIII Augusta* lay at Argentorate and *XXII Primigenia* at Mogontiacum, while on the lower Rhine, *VI Victrix* had moved farther downstream from Novaesium to Vetera, and *I Minervia* returned to its fortress at Bonna. However, the fortress at Noviomagus did not lie empty. There is some evidence that *IX Hispana* occupied the site. Scholars have been unwilling to consider the legion's withdrawal from Britain under Trajan, as this would have left the province with only two legions, but it is possible that *IX Hispana* left Britain shortly after refurbishing the Eburacum fortress in AD 108 (RIB 665).

Meanwhile, in contrast to the blaze of glory in Dacia, the Syrian governor had quietly annexed Arabia (a large area covering present-day Jordan and the Sinai, as well as part of southern Syria), on the death of the reigning client king there. *III Cyrenaica* was transferred up from Egypt to garrison the new praetorian province, and began the construction of a 17ha fortress at Bostra (Bosra, in present-day Syria). However, the relative peace of the east was soon shattered by Trajan's invasion of Parthia in AD 114, for which he assembled a grand army at Satala. Besides the resident legions of Cappadocia and Syria, and *III Cyrenaica* from Arabia, entire units travelled from the Danube, including the Pannonian legions *I* and *II Adiutrix* and *XV Apollinaris*. With only *X Gemina* holding that sector of the Danube front, the elusive *XXX Ulpia* may now have moved to Brigetio, where it has left traces of its presence.

By the end of the year, Trajan began the organization of Armenia as a province, and *IV Scythica* appears to have made a start on the construction of a fortress at Artaxata (AE 1968, 510). AD 115 saw campaigning in Mesopotamia, and early in the following year the emperor stood in the ruins of Ctesiphon, the Parthian capital (near modern Baghdad, Iraq). But rebellion was threatening the rear, and a massive Jewish uprising had begun in Egypt. In a move that was presumably connected with the latter event, a consular governor was installed in Judaea, which (as we have seen) implies an enlarged legionary garrison, and it was surely now that *II Traiana* began construction of a fortress at Caparcotna in Galilee (Megiddo, Israel).

Legionary fortresses under Hadrian (AD 117–138)

On the death of Trajan late in AD 117, the plans to annexe Mesopotamia were shelved, and his successor, Hadrian, began the evacuation of territory beyond the Euphrates. Trouble was again threatening on the Danube, and it must have been a high priority to return legions to their bases. In AD 118/119, Trajan's Dacia was reorganized as three separate commands: two procuratorial provinces, Dacia Inferior in the south and Dacia Porolissensis (named after its capital, Porolissum) in the north, neither with a legionary garrison; and the praetorian province of Dacia Superior, with its single legion, *XIII Gemina*, in the fortress at Apulum. This immediately released *IV Flavia* for a return to Singidunum, rejoining *VII Claudia* in the army of Moesia Superior. There were changes, too, in Pannonia Superior. The retention of *XV Apollinaris* in Cappadocia, to garrison the key fortress at Satala, created a vacancy at Carnuntum; accordingly, *XIV Gemina* marched downriver to occupy this important fortress, and *X Gemina* filled its place at Vindobona.

Our knowledge of the legionary fortresses in the east is woefully inadequate for any period, but particularly for the reign of Hadrian, when one group of

The *porta praetoria* at Lambaesis (Lambèse, Algeria), viewed from inside the fortress. Each carriageway is about 4.5m wide. (R. Cagnat, *Les deux camps de la légion IIIe Auguste à Lambèse d'après les fouilles récentes*, Paris, 1908)

legions seems to have been shuffled back and forth between three or four provinces. The unrest in Egypt had perhaps called for the return of *III Cyrenaica*, for it is attested in AD 119, once more sharing the Nicopolis fortress with *XXII Deiotariana* (BGU 1, 140). Some scholars believe, on the basis of a fragmentary inscription (AE 1983, 937), that *VI Ferrata* now took its place in Arabia, and it is admittedly difficult to find an alternative base for the legion at this time. There is no room for it in Syria: *IV Scythica* remained at Zeugma, and *XVI Flavia*, lately displaced from Satala, took up residence at Samosata, causing (or perhaps following) the transfer of *III Gallica* to Raphanaea (IGLS 4, 1399). Nor is there room in Judaea: *II Traiana* was engaged in road building in Galilee (AE 1989, 744), which seems to confirm its presence at Caparcotna, and the headquarters of *X Fretensis* remained at Jerusalem throughout.

But further moves were afoot. Only a few years later, in AD 123, the threat of war on the Parthian frontier was serious enough to warrant Hadrian's presence in the east, and his military preparations appear to have involved the brigading together of *II Traiana* and *III Cyrenaica* (ILS 5919). If the two legions shared a fortress, the most likely location would have been Egypt, where *II Traiana* had certainly taken up residence by AD 128 (CIL 3, 79); its subsequent long association with Egypt caused Cassius Dio to call it 'the Second Aegyptia legion' (Dio 55.24.3). This would imply a move for *XXII Deiotariana*; but why, and to which fortress? Some scholars, on the other hand, have preferred to place the two legions in neighbouring provinces, *II Traiana* in Egypt and *III Cyrenaica* in Arabia, which in turn implies the movement of *VI Ferrata* out of Arabia and into Judaea. In this scenario, we must still account for *XXII Deiotariana*. In fact, the legion, last attested in AD 119, may already have disappeared from the army list, a casualty of the rioting that is known to have occurred in Alexandria in AD 122 (SHA, *Hadr.* 12.1).

In any event, the outbreak of the so-called Second Jewish War (AD 132–35) saw further disruption amongst the eastern legions. *VI Ferrata* now, if not earlier, garrisoned the Caparcotna fortress, and it, along with *X Fretensis*, bore the brunt of the fighting. In addition, *III Gallica* marched down from Raphanaea in full force, and vexillations were drawn, not only from *II Traiana*, *III Cyrenaica*, and *XII Fulminata*, but from farther afield; elements of *V Macedonica* and *XI Claudia* travelled from Moesia (CIL 3, 14155), and some scholars believe that *IX Hispana* may have accompanied them. When the other legions returned to their home bases, *IX Hispana* (some argue) remained in the east.

Hadrian is chiefly remembered for his personal visits to the provinces of the empire. In AD 128, he visited Africa and Numidia, where *III Augusta* had moved to a new fortress at Lambaesis (Lambèse, Algeria), 100km west of the old base at

Theveste. Six years earlier, he had travelled to Britain, which had recently been the scene of some unrest. Besides a new governor and reinforcements from *VII Gemina*, *VIII Augusta* and *XXII Primigenia* (the legions of Spain and Upper Germany; ILS 2726), the emperor brought a new legion, *VI Victrix* (ILS 1100); it set up its headquarters at Eburacum, which *IX Hispana* had probably vacated years earlier (see p. 27). Meanwhile, the Lower German army was maintained at consular strength by the transfer of *XXX Ulpia* to the Vetera fortress.

Legionary fortresses under the Antonines: Marcus Aurelius and Commodus (AD 161–192)

During the reign of Antoninus Pius (AD 138–161), the various legionary bases did not move from the positions established under Hadrian. By then, only a few key provinces held as many as three legions: Britain, Syria, Upper Pannonia and Lower Moesia. There and elsewhere, fortresses were strung out along the frontiers, and peace was maintained, by and large, for an entire generation. More than one scholar has commented that this was the empire at its height; but in only a few years, it descended into what Edward Gibbon called 'a kingdom of iron and rust'. In AD 161, the new emperor, Marcus Aurelius, was faced with disaster in the east. The Parthian king had occupied the Roman protectorate of Armenia, but inept retaliation by the Cappadocian governor resulted only in his own death and the destruction of a legion at Elegeia (Dio 71.2.1). Most scholars believe that the legion in question must have been *IX Hispana*, although *XXII Deiotariana* is theoretically a possibility, too; certainly, there is no sign of either legion much beyond the AD 120s.

At this time, whole legions could still be mobilized for service on distant frontiers. In response to the Parthian crisis, Marcus sent *I Minervia* from Bonna, *II Adiutrix* from Aquincum, and *V Macedonica* from Troesmis, accompanied by his brother, Lucius Verus, and his military advisors. The ensuing full-scale Roman invasion of Mesopotamia ended in victory in AD 166, but the returning troops brought a plague to the west. In the meantime, Marcus had begun recruiting two new legions; originally named *II Pia* and *III Concors* (e.g., ILS 2287), they were later known as *II* and *III Italica*, underlining the fact that they were recruited in Italy. In the past, the raising of additional legions had gone hand in hand with the annexation of new territory, and it seems that Marcus intended to establish two provinces across the Danube, in Suebian and Sarmatian lands. But Rome's trans-Danubian neighbours were growing restive; pressurized by the migration of Gothic tribes in central Europe, they strained against the frontiers. In AD 170, the Suebian tribes of the Marcomanni and Quadi actually invaded northern Italy, and in subsequent years Marcus moved his headquarters to Carnuntum.

Nomina leg(ionum)		
II Aug(usta)	II Adiut(rix)	IIII Scyth(ica)
VI Victr(ix)	IIII Flav(ia)	XVI Flav(ia)
XX Victr(ix)	VII Claud(ia)	VI Ferrat(a)
VIII Aug(usta)	I Italic(a)	X Frete(nsis)
XXII Prim(igenia)	V Maced(onica)	III Cyren(aica)
I Min(ervia)	XI Claud(ia)	II Traian(a)
XXX Ulp(ia)	XIII Gem(ina)	III Aug(usta)
I Adiut(rix)	XII Fulm(inata)	VII Gem(ina)
X Gem(ina)	XV Apol(linaris)	II Italic(a)
XIIII Gem(ina)	III Gall(ica)	III Italic(a)
I Parth(ica)	II Parth(ica)	III Parth(ica)

The defences of the fortress of Castra Regina (Regensburg), in the Bayern region of Germany, were completed in AD 179. Their massive masonry forms a foundation for medieval rebuilding. (© Florian Himmler)

The situation during the early years of Marcus' reign is confirmed by an inscription at Rome (ILS 2288), which presents, in three columns of text, the names of 33 legions under the general heading 'names of the legions'.

The last entry in each column is one of the three *Parthicae* legions, raised by Septimius Severus in AD 195/7 (see p. 31) and clearly tacked on to the end of the inscription at that time. For the remainder, the list proceeds in an orderly fashion, moving around the Mediterranean province by province, until we reach the bottom of the third column, where the stonemason has added Marcus' two *Italicae* legions. As these are plainly out of geographical sequence, they too must have been an afterthought, demonstrating that, in the main, the list predates their creation in AD 165.

The inscription begins in Britain, where *II Augusta* was based at Isca, *VI Victrix* at Eburacum, and *XX Valeria Victrix* (here simply named *Victrix*) at Deva. Then come the two Germanies, with *VIII Augusta* at Argentorate, *XXII Primigenia* at Mogontiacum, *I Minervia* at Bonna, and *XXX Ulpia* at Vetera. Pannonia Superior is next, with *I Adiutrix* at Brigetio, *X Gemina* at Vindobona, and *XIV Gemina* at Carnuntum. The second column begins with Pannonia Inferior (*II Adiutrix* at Aquincum), followed by the two legions of Moesia Superior (*IV Flavia* at Singidunum and *VII Claudia* at Viminacium), the three legions of Moesia Inferior (*I Italica* at Novae, *V Macedonica* at Troesmis, and *XI Claudia* at Durostorum), and the single legion of Dacia (*XIII Gemina* at Apulum). The list then moves east, with the two legions of Cappadocia (*XII Fulminata* at Melitene and *XV Apollinaris* at Satala), and the middle column ends with the first of the Syrian legions, *III Gallica* (Raphanaea). Column three continues the army of Syria, with *IV Scythica* at Zeugma and *XVI Flavia* at Samosata. Then come the Judaean legions (*VI Ferrata* at Caparcotna and *X Fretensis* at Jerusalem), followed by the single legions of Arabia (*III Cyrenaica* at Bostra), Egypt (*II Traiana* at Nicopolis), Africa (*III Augusta* at Lambaesis) and Spain (*VII Gemina* at Legio).

Marcus' so-called Marcomannic Wars made very little difference to this pattern. In AD 169/170, the Dacian provinces were united as Tres Daciae, 'the three Dacias', under a consular governor, and *V Macedonica* was moved from its base at Troesmis to a new fortress at Potaissa (Turda, Romania). The Marcomanni were defeated in AD 172, the Quadi in AD 173, and the Sarmatian Jazyges in AD 174; when hostilities flared up again in AD 177, Marcus' son Commodus accompanied him on the *expeditio secunda Germanica* ('second German expedition'; AE 1956, 124). The new *legiones Italicae* were no doubt employed in active campaigning during these years, and they were not alone. At one stage, for example, a young senator named Julius Pompilius Piso acted as *praepositus legionibus I Italicae et IIII Flaviae cum omnibus copiis auxiliorum dato iure gladii* ('commander of the first Italian legion and the fourth Flavian legion and all their auxiliary troops, with the power of a governor'; ILS 1111). But the use of vexillations was becoming common, as the career of another young officer demonstrates: at one stage, Valerius Maximianus was given the responsibility of *praepositus vexillationum Leugaricione hiemantium* ('commander of the detachments wintering at Leugaricio'; AE 1956, 124); the vexillations based at Leugaricio (Trencin, Slovakia), 150km into Suebian territory, evidently included elements of *II Adiutrix*.

By now, the balance of power had clearly swung towards the Danube, chiefly at the expense of the Rhine, which was now held by only four legions; by contrast, nine legions were distributed along the Danube, with a tenth in Dacia. The ratio soon became even starker when the two new *Italica* legions settled down on the Danube. In Noricum, *II Italica* had initially occupied the hinterland at Locica (near Celje, Slovenia) before moving up to the frontier *c.* AD 175, to build a fortress at Albing (Austria). In neighbouring Raetia, *III Italica* was engaged in the construction of a fortress at Castra Regina (Regensburg, Germany) in the years running up to AD 179 (CIL 3, 11965). Thus, by AD 180, there were 12 legions along the Danube frontier. The concentration of six of these around the Danube bend is particularly noticeable, with its obvious emphasis on blocking the route from central Europe to Italy and Rome.

Legionary fortresses under the Severans: Septimius Severus and Caracalla (AD 193–217)

Marcus Aurelius died in AD 180, perhaps at Vindobona but definitely on the Danube, directing the military operations there; his son, Commodus, made peace with the northern tribes in order to permit his speedy return to the luxuries of the capital. There was little military activity of any note during his 12-year reign, and his murder, late at night on the last day of AD 192, ushered in a period of civil war. The eventual winner, Septimius Severus (AD 193–208), began preparations for a Parthian campaign by recruiting three new legions named *I*, *II*, and *III Parthica*. But, while two of them accompanied him on the journey to Syria, *II Parthica* founded a fortress at Albanum (present-day Alba, 20km south of Rome). As the first legion to establish a base on Italian soil, it became something of an imperial guard division, accompanying the emperor on campaign; for example, it has left traces of its presence at Apamea (Syria). By AD 198, having overrun the land between the Tigris and the Euphrates, as had Lucius Verus 30 years earlier, Severus established a new province of Mesopotamia in the north. Its administration was modelled on Egypt, so equestrians commanded the two legions, *I Parthica* at Singara (Iraq) and *III Parthica* at Resaina (Turkey). Also during these years, *II Italica* adjusted its position on the Danube by moving 5km west of Albing to Lauriacum (Lorch, Austria); the new fortress was complete by *c.* AD 200.

Severus had risen to power amidst civil war, so it is no surprise that his reign saw further provincial divisions in order to prevent the concentration of troops in the hands of a potential rival. Syria was split into the consular province of Coele, with legions at Samosata and Zeugma, and praetorian Phoenice, with a legion at Raphanaea. Later, Britain was also divided: in the north, Lower Britain (Britannia Inferior) was administered from the fortress at Eburacum, and in the south, the consular governor of Upper Britain (Britannia Superior) controlled the legions at Deva and Isca.

Writing in the early 3rd century AD, Cassius Dio gives a valuable summary of the legionary garrisons of his own day. First, he lists the legions which he believes to have been created by the emperor Augustus (amongst which he mistakenly includes *XXII Primigenia* in Germany):

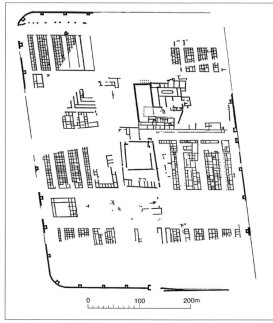

The Second Augusta, which winters in Upper Britain; the three Thirds, the Gallica in Phoenicia, the Cyrenaica in Arabia, and the Augusta in Numidia; the Fourth Scythica in Syria; the Fifth Macedonica in Dacia; the two Sixths, one, the Victrix, stationed in Lower Britain, the other, the Ferrata, in Judaea; the Seventh, generally called Claudia, in Upper Moesia; the Eighth Augusta in Upper Germany; the two Tenths, one, Gemina, in Upper Pannonia, and the other in Judaea; the Eleventh Claudia in Lower Moesia … the Twelfth Fulminata in Cappadocia; the Thirteenth Gemina in Dacia; the Fourteenth Gemina in Upper Pannonia; the Fifteenth in Cappadocia; the Twentieth, called both Valeria and Victrix, in Upper Britain … and the one known as the Twenty-second, which winters in Upper Germany
(Dio 55.23.2–6)

Then, he adds those legions, still in existence in the AD 200s, which had been raised by subsequent emperors:

Nero established the First legion, named Italica, which spends the winter in Lower Moesia; Galba, the First Adiutrix, in Lower Pannonia, and the Seventh Gemina drawn up in Spain; Vespasian, the Second Adiutrix in Lower Pannonia, the Fourth Flavia in Upper Moesia, and the Sixteenth Flavia in Syria; Domitian, the First Minervia in Lower Germany; Trajan, the Second Aegyptia and the Thirtieth Germanica, both of which he named after himself; Marcus Antoninus [i.e., Marcus Aurelius], the Second in Noricum and the Third in Raetia, both of which are named Italica; and Severus, the Parthicae, the First and Third in Mesopotamia, and, in between, the Second in Italy.
(Dio 55.24.2–4)

By this stage, the legionary headquarters had become firmly fixed in their Antonine locations. Even when the province of Dacia was finally given up in AD 274/5, the two legions were evacuated to a newly created province called Dacia Ripensis, in territory previously belonging to the Moesias; *V Macedonica* recommissioned its Flavian fortress at Oescus, and *XIII Gemina* founded a new base at Ratiaria (Archar, Bulgaria).

The elements of a legionary fortress

The overall layout of the fortress

Each legion was probably responsible for the construction of its own fortress. There were various technical specialists in the ranks, from architect-engineers and surveyors to plumbers, roofers, carpenters and stonemasons, all supervised by the *praefectus castrorum* ('prefect of the camp'), an experienced officer promoted after long service as a centurion. In addition, the legionaries would have provided the manpower for clearing the site, assembling the raw materials and building the fortress.

Although no two legionary fortresses are identical, in each case the builders clearly followed a basic blueprint. The perimeter typically enclosed a rectangular area of some 20–25ha, a shape often likened to a playing card. Of course, there were exceptions: in the later 1st century AD, one of the two legions of Germania Inferior was based at Nijmegen, an exceptionally small fortress of only 16.5ha, while the other was based at Bonn, a large square fortress enclosing a massive 27ha. In every fortress, most of the interior was taken up with barrack accommodation, arranged around the centrally located officers' accommodation and administrative buildings. Fresh water was piped in, sometimes by aqueduct, because good hygiene required a steady supply; it has been calculated that an average fortress probably used 200–300m^3 of water a day.

Every fortress had four gateways, one per side. The front gate (*porta praetoria*) and the rear gate (*porta decumana*) lay halfway along each short side. On the long sides, the gateways were positioned about a third of the way along. These side gates, the *portae principales*, were connected by the main lateral road, called the *via principalis* because it ran through the camp past the front of the *principia*. The central position of the *principia* interrupted the main road running longways through the camp, dividing it into a forward length (the *via praetoria*, which led from the *porta praetoria* up to the front of the headquarters) and a rearward length (the *via decumana*, leading to the *porta decumana* at the rear of the fortress). In fact, the *via decumana* ran up to a second transverse street, the *via quintana*, which was not linked to any gateways. These were all fairly major roadways, typically 7–8m wide, metalled with gravel over a bed of cobbles, and cambered, with stone-built side drains; normally, the builders took the opportunity to run sewers underneath, carrying the waste water away from the site. Finally, there was a roadway running around the internal perimeter of the fortress, behind the defences, in the area that Hyginus calls the *intervallum*. This was the *via sagularis*, or 'cloak street', named after the legionary's *sagum*; its purpose was to facilitate the speedy mustering of troops.

The criss-crossing main streets divided the fortress interior into five main zones. The forward area, from the *porta praetoria* down to the *via principalis*, was known as the *praetentura*, and was bisected by the *via praetoria* into a left zone and a right zone. Similarly, the rear area, from the *porta decumana* up to the *via*

It is the fate of most legionary fortresses to have been built over in medieval and later times. The plan of the fortress of Castra Regina (Regensburg, Germany) illustrates this fact. (© Thomas Fischer)

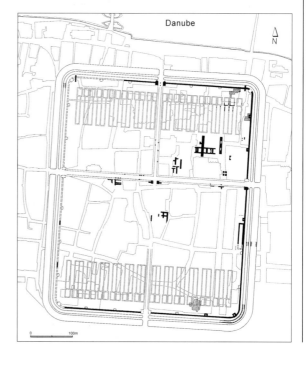

Danube

33

RIGHT A group of visitors enters the south gate (*porta principalis dextra*) of the fortress at Aquincum (Budapest, Hungary). The twin lines of columns mark the edges of the *via principalis*, as it was in the later 2nd century AD. (© Erik Dobat)

BELOW A cistern in the legionary fortress at Tilurium (Gardun). The remains of plaster can be seen sealing the brickwork. Its capacity has been calculated as 10,440 litres. (© M. Sanader)

ABOVE RIGHT In 2004, excavations in the *praetentura* of the fortress at Vindonissa (Windisch, Switzerland) revealed an area of barrack blocks. Here, one of the gravel-surfaced streets separating the individual blocks has been removed, exposing the remains of the earlier timber-phase fortress beneath. The parallel storm drains marking the sides of the street can still be seen. (© Kantonsarchäologie Aargau, Switzerland)

quintana, was known as the *retentura*, and was similarly bisected, this time by the *via decumana*. This left a wide central zone, sandwiched between the *via principalis* and the *via quintana*; it was known as the *latera praetorii*, or 'flanks of the *praetorium*', because the buildings here were arranged around the commander's residence.

In most fortresses, the central zone was two blocks, or *scamna*, deep. One *scamnum* fronted onto the *via principalis*, while the other backed onto the *via quintana*. This can be seen most clearly in the middle, where the *praetorium* usually lay immediately behind the *principia*. It was common for granaries and workshops to occupy plots in this area alongside one of the legion's ten cohorts, but the plot to the right of the *principia* was usually reserved for the prestigious first cohort (see p. 54).

The *retentura* was often only one *scamnum* deep, to accommodate the barracks of four cohorts, laid out with two on either side of the *via decumana*.

Excavations in the 1970s revealed the southern corner of the fortress at Exeter. The clay rampart was fully 6m wide but survived to a height of only 0.9m. About 8m in front lay a massive ditch, 3.8m deep and 4.2m wide (shown here). (© Exeter City Council)

The *praetentura*, on the other hand, was commonly two or three *scamna* deep. The first of these, like the *retentura*, contained the barrack blocks of four cohorts. But the hospital and baths might take up much of the remaining space. One *scamnum* in particular, fronting the *via principalis*, was reserved for the higher officers' houses (see p. 50).

The massive 2m-thick walls of Castra Regina (Regensburg), still standing around 8m high, were originally fronted by two 3m-deep ditches, one 7m wide and the other 16m wide. (© Florian Himmler)

The defences

Developing from the temporary field fortifications of the legions on campaign, the earliest fortresses were defended by a turf rampart, fronted by one or more ditches. It seems that, as time progressed, a single v-shaped ditch became the norm, usually around 2m deep and 5–6m wide; the 8m-wide ditch at Caerleon was exceptional. The material extracted from the ditch was normally thrown

Aerial view of the south corner of the fortress at Mirebeau (France), with the buried stonework showing as parched lines in the field. The square interval towers can clearly be seen astride the rampart. (© Archéologie aérienne René Goguey)

The fortress wall at Deva (Chester, England) survives, on the north side, up to the level of the walkway, as indicated by the moulded cornice, visible here. The method of construction was known as *opus quadratum*, in which large blocks of stone, up to 1.8m long, were laid without mortar. The work is thought to date from around AD 100. (© M. C. Bishop)

out to form a low, flat-topped counterscarp bank; only rarely was it utilized in the rampart make-up.

In fortresses of the 1st century AD, the rampart was principally of stacked turves with some admixture of earth and gravel. From a base 4–5m wide, it was battered at the front and rear to provide a 2m-wide rampart-walk at a height of around 3m. Scholars have periodically suggested that there was a standard fortress blueprint, marked out in Roman feet (1 Rf = 29.5cm), and it may have been normal practice for the surveyors to mark out a linear zone for the rampart, 20 Roman feet (*c*.6m) wide. At any rate, it has been calculated that, for the average 20ha fortress, the entire area must have been stripped of turf, in order to provide enough material for the rampart, which typically ran for over 1.8km. No doubt, the rampart was surfaced with a timber corduroy walkway, and provided with a timber breastwork at the front and some kind of safety rail at the rear.

Once the turf had become sufficiently compacted, in a process that probably took months, it became common practice from the mid-1st century AD to trim back the front batter, creating a vertical face against which a stone wall was built. At Inchtuthil, this wall was approximately 5 Rf (1.5m) thick, faced with massive pink sandstone blocks 0.6m long and 0.25m high; at Chester, even larger blocks 1.8m long and over 1m wide were used, and the result must have been particularly impressive. The visual effect was perhaps important to the Roman builders, who appear to have used a pinkish-coloured mortar at Caerleon, binding the light-coloured blocks of the curtain wall. The stone wall would have been carried up to form a parapet, perhaps 1.5m high and 1m thick; the remaining width, rather narrow for a functional wallwalk, was of course supplemented by the existing 2m-wide rampart-walk, which was probably at this stage flagged in stone. The entire building process was undoubtedly a long one; it has been calculated, for example, that the curtain wall of the Chester fortress required 40,000 blocks of stone to be quarried, dressed, transported and laid.

Timber towers originally flanked the four gateways; others were often positioned at all four corners and at regular intervals along each side. The lower

The foundations of an interval tower on the north rampart of the fortress at Mirebeau (near Dijon, France). The square structure is 4.80m wide, and must have risen at least as high as the rampart, which is thought to have stood 5m high. (© Michel Reddé)

The *principia* at the centre of the Flavian fortress at Mirebeau (France), showing from the air in 1964 as a crop mark. (© Archéologie aérienne René Goguey)

storey of the gate towers was probably boarded in, to provide guard chambers, but elsewhere, the towers would have consisted of four massive corner posts, supporting a platform some way above the rampart. The evidence of Trajan's Column suggests that the upper levels of towers were left open, perhaps to reduce wind resistance; it is not certain whether or not they were roofed, although this would have been advisable in northern Europe. Such defences may appear temporary to the modern observer, but the Romans perceived them to be permanent. Of course, they required constant maintenance, which eventually made construction in stone more attractive. Rebuilding in stone would also have afforded the opportunity of roofing any previously unroofed towers.

The headquarters building (*principia*)

The headquarters building (*principia*) occupied a central position in each fortress, and followed a formal layout, based on the forum of a Roman town. It was entered through a monumental gate structure, known as the *groma* because this was the position of the surveyors' reference point (see p. 7). Inside, there

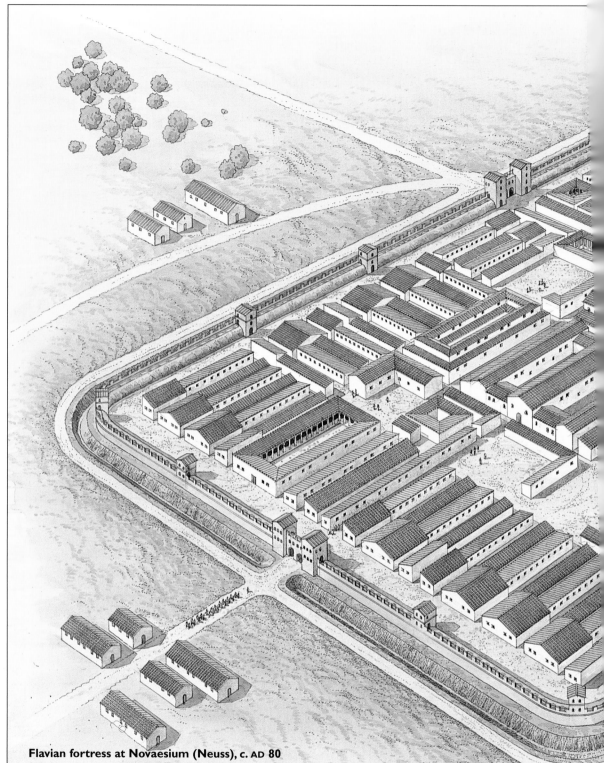

Flavian fortress at Novaesium (Neuss), c. AD 80
Strategically placed on a high ground near the west bank of the Rhine, the site at Neuss was occupied by Roman troops from the reign of Augustus onwards. Ten distinct chronological periods have been identified. The earth-and-timber fortress that succeeded earlier encampments was destroyed in AD 69, and rebuilt in stone by legion *VI Victrix*. But it remained in occupation for only around 35 years, after which it was demolished to make room for

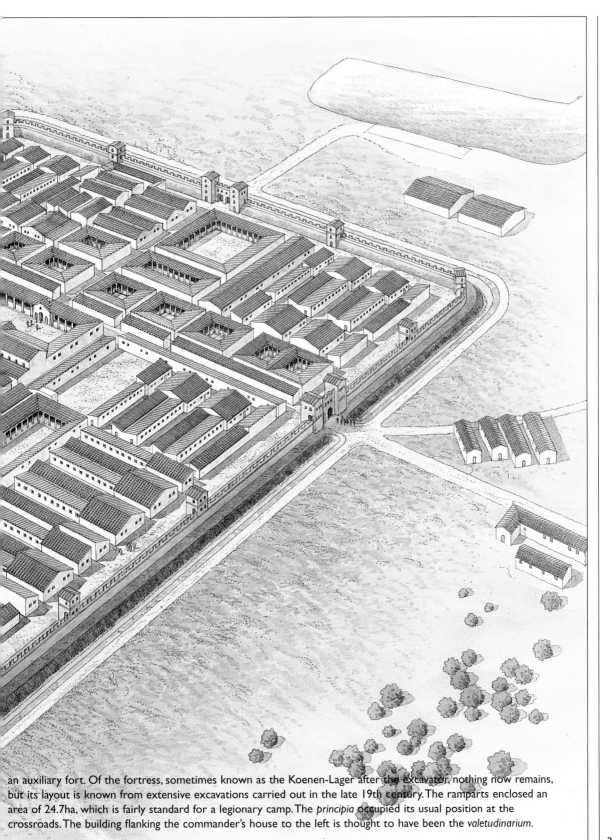

an auxiliary fort. Of the fortress, sometimes known as the Koenen-Lager after the excavator, nothing now remains, but its layout is known from extensive excavations carried out in the late 19th century. The ramparts enclosed an area of 24.7ha, which is fairly standard for a legionary camp. The *principia* occupied its usual position at the crossroads. The building flanking the commander's house to the left is thought to have been the *valetudinarium*.

The monumental tetrapylon (four-way arch) at Lambaesis spans the *via principalis* and marks the entrance to the *principia*. The associated inscription (CIL 8, 2571) indicates that it was called the *groma*. (R. Cagnat, *Les deux camps de la légion IIIe Auguste à Lambèse d'après les fouilles récentes*, Paris, 1908)

The cross-hall of the *principia* at El-Lejjun has a raised *tribunal* (platform) at either end. The commanding officer would mount the platform by a staircase, the remains of which can be seen in the foreground of this photograph. (© Gregory Linton/Karak Resources Project)

was an open, colonnaded courtyard, commonly surrounded by a gutter to collect rainwater from the pitched roof; this often fed into a water tank, such as the one found at Inchtuthil which had a capacity of 47,500 litres! The courtyard was surrounded on three sides by rows of rooms, thought to be armouries (*armamentaria*) and other stores. An inscription from Lambaesis indicates the existence of an *armamentarium* somewhere within the *principia* (ILS 2437), and weapons have been discovered at this location in other fortresses. The fourth side of the courtyard was occupied by a long cross-hall (*basilica*), designed as an assembly hall with a tribunal at one, or sometimes each, end.

Behind the *basilica*, a series of offices (*officia*) flanked the central shrine (*aedes*), where the legion's eagle standard (*aquila*) and the 59 centurial standards (*signa*) were kept. On account of this, the building clearly had religious overtones, as shown by the frequent finds of altars during excavation. The standard-bearers of the Roman army had financial responsibilities, too. Consequently, in many fortresses, the floor of the central shrine was elevated to create a strongroom (*aerarium*) in the basement, where the official legionary funds and the soldiers' savings could be kept safely. Various clerks probably occupied the other offices, processing the mountain of documentation that each legion generated (e.g., Veg., *de re mil.* 2.19). One room at Lambaesis contained an inscription confirming that it was the *tabularium legionis* ('records office of the legion'; ILS 9100), and that the staff of the adjutant (*cornicularius*) based there included a registrar (*actarius*) and several secretaries (*librarii*). Some of the rooms at Novae had seating along the walls. This kind of evidence, along with inscriptions from Lambaesis, suggests that some of them were used as meeting rooms (*scholae*) for the various guilds (*collegia*) of minor officers. However, such guilds are not thought to predate the mid-2nd century AD.

Everything points to the fact that the *principia* was the hub of the fortress. It was the religious centre, where the spirit of the legion resided (in the form of the *aquila*); and it was the administrative centre, where the official records were processed, where sums of money were collected and disbursed, and where large numbers of troops could assemble for an address by the commanding officer. No doubt, the monumentality of the building and its rich decoration added to the sense of ceremony.

Other buildings

Each fortress was a self-contained military town. Although the greater part of its area was occupied by accommodation for the men and their officers, many other types of building were regularly included. For the modern observer, some of these defy explanation. For example, the main streets in many fortresses were lined with open-fronted cubicles, which scholars frequently classify as *tabernae*, a catch-all label for a booth or a cabin. The *tabernae* lining the *via principalis* at Vindonissa contained broken pottery, so it is likely that they had been used as storerooms. Others may have been offices or small workshops.

The workshops (*fabricae*)

Many legionaries were excused from the usual round of fatigues because they practised a particular craft or skill; such men were known as *immunes*. Many of these crafts were linked to the manufacture and repair of equipment, which must have been carried out in large workshops. Indeed, one papyrus from Egypt refers to work *in fabricam legionis* ('in the legionary workshop; P. Berlin 6765). Such buildings probably took a variety of forms. In his study of legionary buildings, the German archaeologist Harald von Petrikovits identified three likely types: the long, rectangular hall; the 'double hook' or U-shaped building; and the 'bazaar-type' complex, characterized by a maze of interconnected rooms. But the use to which the buildings were put is not always obvious. For example, a U-shaped building at Lambaesis was interpreted as a wheelwright's shop because two stone-cut channels, running out onto the road, had the same track width as wheel ruts found on the *via praetoria*. However, without evidence of industrial activity, the building's purpose must remain uncertain.

At Exeter and Inchtuthil, large courtyard buildings have been identified as *fabricae* on the basis of industrial debris. It was in the building at Inchtuthil that the excavator Sir Ian Richmond found the well-known hoard of a million nails and nine iron tyres, buried when the fortress was abandoned, and a smithing hearth stood nearby. A similarly sized courtyard building in the *retentura* at Caerleon may have been a *fabrica*, as it was associated with

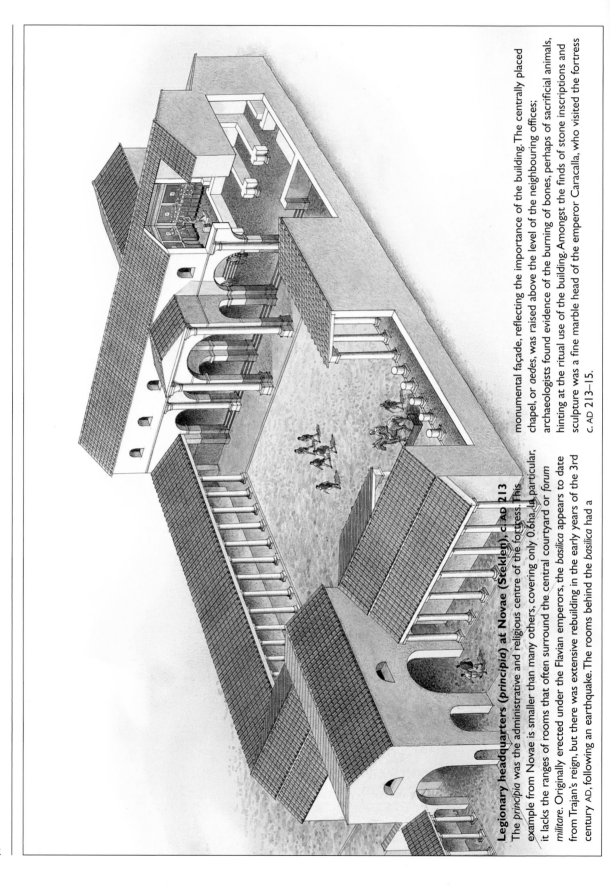

Legionary headquarters (principia) at Novae (Steklen), c. AD 213

The *principia* was the administrative and religious centre of the fortress. This example from Novae is smaller than many others, covering only 0.6ha. In particular, it lacks the ranges of rooms that often surround the central courtyard or *forum militare*. Originally erected under the Flavian emperors, the *basilica* appears to date from Trajan's reign, but there was extensive rebuilding in the early years of the 3rd century AD, following an earthquake. The rooms behind the *basilica* had a monumental façade, reflecting the importance of the building. The centrally placed chapel, or *aedes*, was raised above the level of the neighbouring offices; archaeologists found evidence of the burning of bones, perhaps of sacrificial animals, hinting at the ritual use of the building. Amongst the finds of stone inscriptions and sculpture was a fine marble head of the emperor Caracalla, who visited the fortress c. AD 213–15.

lead-working refuse. Of course, there were many other trades besides smithing within the ranks of the legion, and many fortresses must have had workshops for leatherworking, woodworking and glassmaking, to name only three.

The hospital (*valetudinarium*)

Sick or injured legionaries were cared for in a hospital building. Hyginus recommended that it should be located as far as possible from the workshops, 'in order to ensure quiet for the convalescents', but there was no standard position within the fortress. For example, at Caerleon, Vetera, Novae and,

The site of the *principia* at Novae (Steklen, Bulgaria), viewed from the south-west corner. In the foreground, two of the rear rooms can be seen, fronting onto the cross-hall (*basilica principiorum*). The area of the courtyard (*forum militare*) lies under woodland, but archaeological sampling has elucidated much of the plan.
(© Martin Lemke)

The hospital (*valetudinarium*) at Novae (Steklen, Bulgaria), looking north along the main corridor. To left and right, there is a recurring pattern of two wards separated by a small vestibule. The river Danube can be seen in the background.
(© Martin Lemke)

probably, Lauriacum the hospital lay in the *praetentura*, while a site in the right *latus praetorii* was selected at Inchtuthil, Neuss, Carnuntum and Bonn.

The building always followed the same plan, in which two rows of rooms, separated by a corridor, ran around the four sides of an open, collonaded courtyard. Most of the rooms were arranged in pairs of wards flanking a small vestibule, which gave access to the corridor; the vestibule gave the wards a degree of privacy, while the corridor permitted staff to circulate around the hospital. The average room size of 15–20m² could comfortably have accommodated four sick beds. At Novae, there is evidence that the wards each had two large windows opening to the outside, so that the patients could enjoy fresh air, and the floors were apparently covered with fine sand. Evidence of under-floor heating (hypocaust) was found at Caerleon, while the hospital at Vetera had a small baths suite and latrine. Scholars have often commented on the apparent provision of 60-odd wards, corresponding to the *centuriae* of the legion, but it seems unlikely that each *centuria* had a designated ward.

The *valetudinarium* at Neuss produced dozens of medical instruments, including probes, hooks and scalpels, and in several hospitals, a large hall, sometimes centrally located near the entrance, has been interpreted as an operating theatre. Not all of the remaining rooms were arranged as wards. Some, at the corners and elsewhere, were probably intended as storerooms for the various medicines and potions: the lid of a medicine box, labelled *ex radice britanica* ('extract of British root'; AE 1929, 102), was found at Haltern, while wine barrels discovered at Aquincum were stamped IMMVNE IN R VAL LEG II AD, an abbreviation of *immune in rationem valetudinarii legionis II Adiutricis* ('duty free for the account of the hospital of legion *II Adiutrix*'; AE 1933, 120). Other rooms were probably offices, for the hospital, like the other major buildings in the fortress, had its own staff, under the general direction of the *praefectus castrorum*. The hospital orderlies, like the workers in the *fabricae*, were probably *immunes*, but the skilled medical personnel no doubt ranked as *principales*, whose special responsibilities entitled them to increased pay. The *optio valetudinarii* was perhaps in charge of the day-to-day running of the hospital; two of these officers are known from Aquincum, where they made dedications to the health deities Hygeia and Telesphoros (AE 1937, 181; 1955, 13). A shrine to Aesculapius, god of medicine, stood in the courtyard at Novae, and it has been suggested that, in legionary fortresses, the entire hospital was viewed as a religious sanctuary of sorts.

The granaries (*horrea*)

The daily rations of the legionaries were stored in buildings that had a distinctive design, related to the nature of their contents. They took the form of long rectangular barns with thick walls, strengthened by external buttresses; some of the areas between the buttresses were perhaps louvred for ventilation. The internal flooring, sometimes flagstones and sometime wooden planking, was raised above ground level on pillars or sleeper walls, creating a shallow basement that was open to draughts.

The name 'granary' is misleading, inasmuch as all manner of foodstuffs were stored there. Although the soldier's staple food was cereal, either corn or wheat, archaeology has turned up evidence, at Vindonissa and elsewhere, for the consumption of meat, poultry, oysters, snails and fish; wine and olive oil were imported, and various types of vegetables were eaten. Some of this would have been supplied fresh for immediate consumption, but some would have been stored in the granary buildings.

Tacitus claims that the garrisons established in Britain in AD 79 had 'supplies to last for a year' (*Agr.* 22.2), and it has been calculated that, annually, a legion would have consumed approximately 2,000 tonnes of corn and wheat alone. Some scholars have suggested that, inside the individual granaries, a system of wooden hoppers was installed to contain loose grain; this, they argue, would have created massive lateral thrust, necessitating the external buttresses that characterise these buildings. However, such foodstuffs would have been more easily manhandled in sacks. It is more likely that the buttresses were primarily intended to bear the weight of the heavy tiled roof and to carry the eaves far out beyond the walls to remove the risk of dampness; a secondary function was perhaps to compensate for the weakening of the side walls wherever they were louvred for additional ventilation.

Even the granaries had their own administration. The *dispensator horreorum* ('steward of the granaries'), known from Mainz (CIL 13, 11802) and Viminacium (AE 1973, 471), presumably looked after the storage of supplies there, while the *horrearius* mentioned on an inscription at Rome (ILS 2160) probably had a similar job. And the all-pervasive Roman religion extended into this area, for it appears that, on occasion, the *genius horreorum* ('guardian spirit of the granaries'; AE 1924, 34) had to be mollified.

The remains of a large building at Tilurium. Such heavy buttressing is normally indicative of a granary (*horreum*), with its heavy roof projecting out beyond the walls. (© M. Sanader)

The baths (*thermae*)

Every fortress was provided with a baths complex (*thermae*) for the use of the troops. These were generally built of masonry, even in the turf-and-timber fortresses of the early period, no doubt to reduce the risk of fire from the building's massive furnaces, while preventing deterioration from dampness and maintaining constant temperatures in the various rooms. Unlike the headquarters and the commander's residence, the baths had no

Roman baths (*thermae*) were arranged around the basic sequence of cold room (*frigidarium*), warm room (*tepidarium*), and hot room (*caldarium*). At Caerleon, part of the first of these has been preserved and can still be seen. The architecturally demanding design of the building, pioneered by military engineers in a succession of fortresses, reached its zenith in the great baths buildings at Rome. With thousands of soldiers accommodated in the fortress, visits to the baths must have been regulated in some way, but we know nothing of the system. The visitor could exercise in the open courtyard and swim in the 40m pool (*natatio*), or make use of the covered hall (*basilica*), before entering the suite of rooms for the traditional cleansing process. Visits to the baths are thought to have been social occasions, too, with leisurely chatter and gaming.

Ruins of the bath complex (*thermae*) at El-Lejjun (Jordan), built in the *praetentura*, against the northern wall of the fortress. (© Gregory Linton/Karak Resources Project)

fixed location within a fortress, but they were often sited in the *praetentura* and, perhaps more importantly, near the hospital, emphasizing the connection between health and cleanliness. In the fortress at Inchtuthil, for example, a vacant area across the street from the hospital had probably been reserved for the baths. As the largest structure in each fortress, the *thermae* represented a real feat of engineering; at Caerleon, the vaulted ceilings probably soared 15m above the floor and the entire complex covered an area of almost 1ha.

In Roman culture, bathing had a recreational and social function. The excavator of Caerleon, George Boon, quoted an inscription from Africa that neatly sums up the legionary's philosophy: *venari, lavari, ludere, ridere, hoc est vivere* ('to hunt, to bathe, to gamble, to laugh, this is living'; CIL 8, 17938, adapted). These priorities were partly satisfied by incorporating an outdoor exercise yard (*palaestra*), often with open-air swimming pool (*natatio*). In their ingenuity, the Roman engineers normally ensured that the *palaestra* was laid out to the south of the baths complex, to maximize on warmth and sunlight, and to avoid the massive building's shadow. Furthermore, the *thermae* in the fortresses of the chilly north-west also had indoor exercise halls (*basilicae thermarum*), no doubt in case of inclement weather; the example at Caerleon was *c*.60m long and over 20m wide, and the one at Chester even had its own indoor swimming pool.

The main baths building comprised the essential components of the Roman bathing process. Besides the changing room (*apodyterium*), there were three main halls, laid out in sequence: the first, called the *frigidarium* (cold room), was unheated, and usually incorporated one or more cold-water wash basins

Legionary baths complex at Isca (Caerleon), c. AD 150

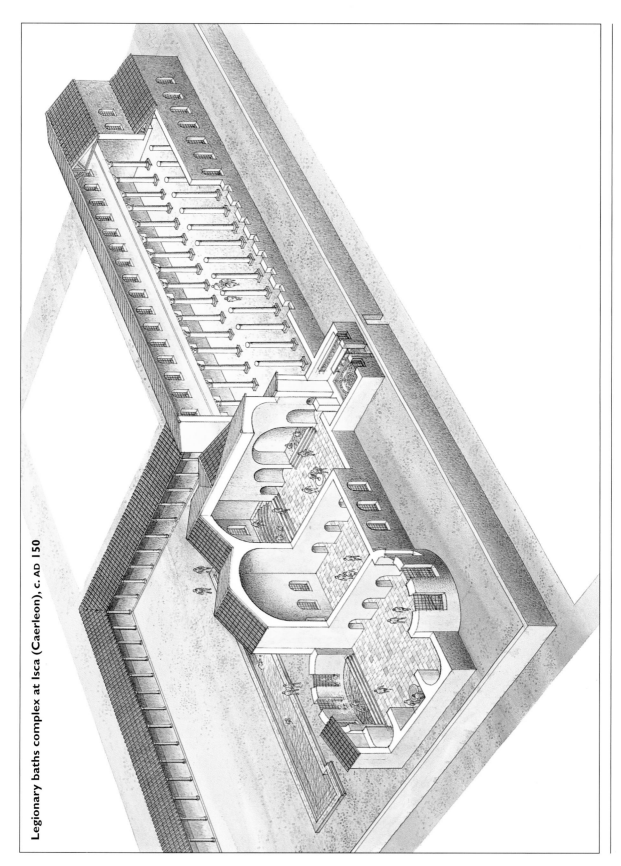

The hot room (*caldarium*) of the baths in the Neronian fortress at Exeter (England). The underfloor heating (hypocaust) appears as a grid of small pillars, originally supporting the floor of the hot room. (© Exeter City Council)

(*labra*) and plunge pools (*piscinae*); the second, called the *tepidarium* (warm room), was moderately heated; and the third, the *caldarium* (hot room), often incorporated a hot-water pool. The bather progressed through the increasing temperatures, to induce a cleansing perspiration, at which point dirt and grime could be scraped from his oiled body using a bronze tool called a strigil; a final cold plunge had the effect of closing the pores. The bathing process could be further refined by including a *sudatorium* (sweat room); this chamber, sometimes called a *laconicum*, provided the dry heat of the modern sauna, in contrast to the steamy atmosphere of the *caldarium*, found in the modern Turkish baths. A broadly similar arrangement of rooms existed in the fortresses of Europe – for example, Exeter, Caerleon, Neuss, Vindonissa, Lauriacum – but an altogether different plan was followed for the *thermae* at Lambaesis, where the different climate called for increased provision of cold facilities.

Finds of jewellery trapped in the drainage system often prompt the suggestion that women frequented the baths. Although the 88 gemstones recovered from the silt of the *frigidarium* drain at Caerleon probably came from soldiers' rings, silver hairpins from the same site are considered more feminine. Of course, wives often accompanied centurions and the higher officers on their tour of duty, and it seems reasonable to suggest that women were permitted to use the facilities at particular times.

Living in a legionary fortress

The internal structure of the legion

The fortress was, in theory, the home of the entire legion. Although no ancient author ever states the normal strength of a legion, there was a widely held belief that it numbered around 6,000 men. As just one example, Pompey was known to have crossed from Italy to Macedonia in 49 BC with five legions (Caes., *BCiv*. 3.4.1), which Cicero reckoned as 30,000 soldiers (Cic., *Att*. 9.6.3). Such a shorthand figure perhaps arose from the knowledge that the legion consisted of 60 centuries (*centuriae*), and the name 'century' implies 100 men. However, the evidence is ambiguous: both Appian and Plutarch describe Caesar's 13th legion, marching on Rome in 49 BC, as '5,000 infantry and 300 cavalry' (App., *B Civ*. 2.32; Plut., *Caes*. 32; *Pomp*. 60).

Although a unit's strength might fluctuate during periods of warfare, its full complement should have been guaranteed accommodation in a winter base. According to Hyginus, legionaries on campaign were organized into tent-parties (*contubernia*) of eight men. In the camp, each *contubernium* was assigned a plot of ground to accommodate the tent (10 Rft square = 3m²), with extra space in front for the men to stack their equipment. Ten *contubernia* formed a century (*centuria*), which was thus theoretically 80-men strong, and camped in a row with the centurion's tent at one end. It was usual for two centuries to encamp in rows facing each other across a narrow lane; Hyginus says that they were assigned a strip of ground (*striga*) 120 Rft long by 60 Rft wide (35.5 x 17.8m). These pairs of facing *centuriae* were grouped in blocks of three, which made up the legionary cohort. (A legion was divided into ten cohorts, each comprising six centuries, although Hyginus complicates matters by informing us that the first cohort was of double strength.) In a permanent fortress, it is logical to assume that individual centuries occupied single barrack buildings, and indeed one inscription (RIB 334) suggests that such buildings were known as *centuriae*. Furthermore, patterns of six barrack blocks can often be identified archaeologically, apparently corresponding to individual cohorts. And finally, as we shall see (see p. 53), the design of the typical barrack building incorporated more spacious accommodation at one end, corresponding to the large tent of the centurion.

Besides the men and their centurions, there were eight officers to be accommodated in the fortress. The commander himself, styled the *legatus legionis* ('legate of the legion'), was a senator of middling seniority en route to a consulship and the major provincial governorships. By the mid-1st century AD, when the career system had finally settled down, legionary commands were only open to men who had served as *praetor* at Rome, a post normally held by 30-year-olds. Thus, the same man was qualified to govern a one-legion 'praetorian' province like Numidia.) As commander, the legate was assisted by a young man just embarking on a senatorial career; he was

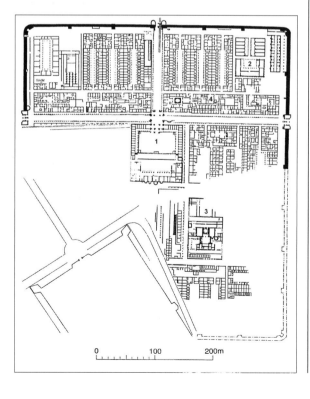

Plan of the legionary fortress at Lambaesis (Lambèse, Algeria), founded by *III Augusta* during the reign of Hadrian but extensively rebuilt in the AD 250s. The construction of a French prison in the late 19th century obliterated the south-west quadrant. Amongst the surviving buildings are the famous *thermae* (3), the *scamnum tribunorum* (4), and a possible *fabrica* (2). (© Dietwulf Baatz)

0   100   200m

technically termed the *tribunus laticlavius* ('broad-stripe tribune'), referring to the wide purple stripe which adorned the senator's tunic. Both the legate and the tribune might spend a three-year tour of duty, before moving on to the next stage in their careers. Third in seniority was the *praefectus castrorum*, a man whose long service as a centurion had culminated in the accolade of *primus pilus* (chief centurion); as prefect, he served out his last 12 months with the legion in general charge of the camp infrastructure. Ranked beneath him were the five equestrian tribunes, the *tribuni angusticlavii* ('narrow-stripe tribunes'), whose largely administrative duties reflected the fact that many incumbents had already attained high civil office in their hometowns and wished only a taste of the army. Others might already have spent three or four years in command of an auxiliary cohort, and perhaps envisaged a long military career leading one day to the coveted praetorian prefecture at Rome. Whichever career path they followed, the equestrian tribunes had one thing in common: their social status was closer by far to the two senatorial officers than to any of the legionary soldiers under their command.

The commander's house (*praetorium*)

The accommodation provided for the officers differed markedly from that of the ordinary soldiers. In the marching camp, the commander's tent was located in the centre. The same layout was retained in the fortress, where the *praetorium* was normally sited beside, or more commonly behind, the *principia*. The fortress of Inchtuthil was abandoned before construction work had begun on the *praetorium*, but the excavator, Sir Ian Richmond, believed that it would have occupied the vacant area beside the *principia*; it is, of course, equally likely that the area to the rear had been earmarked for the commander's residence. This is certainly the position occupied by the building in the fortresses at Neuss, Caerleon, Carnuntum and, probably, Nijmegen, while in the double fortress at Vetera the two *praetoria* flanked the *principia*.

As the dwelling of a fairly high-ranking senator, who was probably accompanied on his tour of duty by his family, this building followed the plan of a luxurious Roman house; indeed, scholars often refer to the building as the legate's palace. Besides living rooms and gardens for the family's use, the *praetorium* had to have servants' quarters and public rooms, where the senator could meet his fellow officers and entertain distinguished visitors; it is quite likely that he had his own baths suite, as well. Unfortunately, few legionary *praetoria* are known in any detail, but the residence of *V Alaudae*'s legate in the western half of Vetera provides a splendid example, where the hippodrome-shaped garden is particularly striking.

On the subject of *praetoria*, von Petrikovits lamented the fact that we lack a complete plan of a fortress from one of the one-legion provinces; the significance, of course, is that the legionary commander was also the provincial governor, and perhaps his residence was sited elsewhere.

The tribunes' houses (*domūs*)

The commander's immediate subordinates, the prefect and six tribunes, had their own houses. Their accommodation commonly lay in the *praetentura*, where it took the form of a strip of land along the *via principalis*; this was known as the *scamnum tribunorum*. Little is known of this area in the fortress at Caerleon, but several houses have been excavated at Vindonissa, Carnuntum, Inchtuthil and Lambaesis. In fact, the latter is the only example where the entire *scamnum tribunorum* is known; unfortunately, the number of individual houses is unclear because they are not formally separated, but there appear to be seven. The westernmost is far larger and more luxurious than the others, and was probably the *domus* of the *tribunus laticlavius*, although the excavator preferred the house opposite the *principia*, at the corner of the *viae praetoria* and *principalis dextra*.

Tribunes' houses, like this one in the legionary fortress at Aquincum (Budapest, Hungary), were designed around a central courtyard in the 'peristyle' manner. (© Erik Dobat)

Barracks 2 and 3 in the west corner of the fortress at Caerleon lie back to back. In the foreground lie the spacious quarters allocated to the centurion of each block. (© Author)

The prefect and the tribunes required lodgings to match their elevated social standing. They were each attended by servants, and may well have been accompanied by their families; certainly, during the reign of Commodus, the *praefectus castrorum* at Bonn made a dedication with his three sons to the *genius domūs* ('guardian spirit of the house'; CIL 13, 8016).

The houses themselves followed the Mediterranean design, with rooms arranged around a colonnaded courtyard; this central space was technically known as a *peristylium*, and was probably laid out as a garden. Each house had the all-important dining room (*triclinium*), where the officer could entertain his peers, and a kitchen for the preparation of meals. At Inchtuthil, Neuss and, perhaps, Nijmegen, there were rooms obviously set aside for administration, but this is only to be expected, as each officer had his own staff (*officium*). An inscription set up at Lambaesis during the reign of Septimius Severus names the adjutant (*cornicularius*) and 11 assistants (*beneficiarii*) belonging to the senatorial tribune (ILS 2397); the staff of the prefect in the same fortress included secretaries (*librarii*) and accountants (*numerarii*) (AE 1899, 60).

The barrack blocks (*centuriae*)

The most numerous structure in any Roman military base was the barrack, which was laid out as a long, narrow building, emulating the row of soldiers'

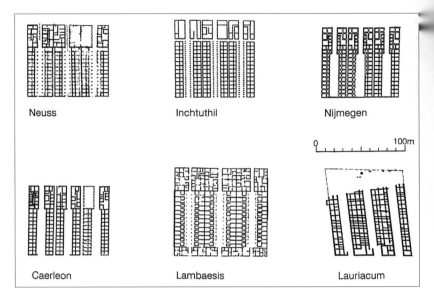

Neuss   Inchtuthil   Nijmegen

0   100m

Caerleon   Lambaesis   Lauriacum

tents in a temporary camp. Individual barracks were grouped in blocks of three facing pairs, each pair separated by an alleyway. The resulting cluster of six, separated from neighbouring groups by alleyways, corresponded to the legionary cohort. They were sited close to the edges of the fortress so that, in theory, the soldiers could man the defences quickly if attacked.

For roughly two-thirds of its length, each barrack consisted of a double row of rooms, fronted by a continuous veranda. Usually 2–3m deep, this served as a sheltered area, perhaps for drying off and shedding equipment before entering the building. Many verandas show evidence of rubbish pits, sunk into the ground and perhaps lined with a removable wicker basket; examples from Inchtuthil contained food refuse. Other such pits contained small nails, indicating an original timber cover or lining, and were perhaps used as emergency latrines. Although communal latrines that flushed into the main sewer (at least in rainy weather) were probably a feature of every fortress, they were perhaps difficult to access in the dead of night.

In every barrack, the outer room, opening onto the veranda, corresponded to the men's equipment space in the temporary camp, and is often called the *arma* ('weapons') for that reason; the larger, inner room corresponded to the *contubernium* tent, or *papilio*. The total space for each eight-man unit averaged 30m². For example, in the barracks at Aquincum, many *contubernia* measured 3.50 × 3.50m (*arma*) and 4.50 × 3.50m (*papilio*). The figures from Caerleon are broadly similar, averaging 3.40 × 4.00m (*arma*) and 4.30 × 4.00m (*papilio*). Floors were commonly of compacted clay, but *opus signinum*, a kind of concrete mixed with crushed tile, was used at Caerleon, Vindonissa and Carnuntum, and evidence of timber flooring was found at Chester.

Where archaeology has recovered only the foundations of barrack buildings, it is a challenge to imagine what they must have looked like. There were evidently windows, judging from finds of glass at Caerleon and Carnuntum, but it is unlikely that these were in the rear room, as the individual blocks generally backed onto one another. One possibility is to imagine a stepped roof, where the front room was roofed at a lower level than the rear room, creating a clerestory between the two. A common internal feature was an open hearth, which must have been particularly welcome in the chilly north-west. Examples studied at Chester consisted of a semicircular kerb of stones, projecting from the wall and enclosing a thick tiled hearth; a brick flue perhaps carried the smoke up and out of the roof. By contrast, at Caerleon, the excavator was struck by the complete absence of hearths in the barracks, and proposed that portable braziers must have been used instead. Whatever the source of heating (and incidental lighting), it would surely have been possible to cook in the barrack room. Each *contubernium* perhaps had a quern for the men to grind their own ration, before making it into bread and baking it in the communal ovens; if they chose to make porridge instead, it could easily have been heated on the barrack hearth.

Logically, we might expect groups of eight men to have shared a barrack room, just as they shared a tent, but the archaeological evidence is seldom as clear cut. Barracks at Caerleon, Neuss and Aquincum, for example, were divided into 12 pairs of rooms, whereas ten would have sufficed; barracks investigated at Inchtuthil even had 14. Either there were fewer than eight men in each *contubernium*, or the spare rooms had some other function. In fact, it is possible that extra space was allocated to the *principales* (or junior officers) who served under the centurion; namely, the *signifer* (standard-bearer), the *optio* (the centurion's 'chosen' deputy), and the *tesserarius* (the 'tablet bearer', who was in charge of the watchword). Some of these may have required office space to carry out their paperwork, but it is quite likely that their enhanced pay grade entitled them to more generous living quarters. As in other buildings of the fortress, religion was never far away. A small marble plinth, dedicated to the *genius signiferorum* ('guardian spirit of the standard-bearers'), was found in a barrack room at Chester; the dedicator, Titus Flavius Valerianus, 'gave it as

The buildings tucked into the north-west rampart at Caerleon include a latrine (foreground), presumably for the use of the men accommodated in the near-by barrack blocks. (© Author)

a gift to his colleagues' (RIB 451). Another dedication, found near the barracks at Vindobona, read *in honorem genii centuriae* ('in honour of the guardian spirit of the barracks'; AE 2001, 1656).

The men's accommodation accounted for only around two-thirds of the building's length; the remaining third belonged to the centurion. The barrack was usually oriented so that the centurion's quarters lay on the *via sagularis* or, more rarely (and only for any barracks in the *latera praetorii*), on the *via principalis*. With no veranda, his quarters took up the full width of the building, and comprised several rooms arranged around a central corridor. The resulting living space was typically 300m^2, or ten times as large as one of the *contubernia*. Of course, this reflected the centurion's position and status. It is true that many centurions had risen from the ranks, and thus came from the same humble backgrounds as the ordinary soldiers, but many had been promoted after 16 years' service in the Praetorian Guard; others were equestrians who had entered the centurionate in preference to the usual career structure of their peers. The social gulf that separated them from their men was reflected in their salary, which was probably ten or 12 times as much as the ordinary legionary's; it is not surprising to find that they lived in relative luxury.

The general design of the centurions' quarters suggests that, unlike the higher officers in their *domūs*, the centurions were not expected to entertain.

Barrack blocks usually clustered in groups of six, which presumably corresponded to the legionary cohort. The L-shaped plan is typical, with more spacious accommodation at one end, usually nearest the rampart. By analogy with the situation in temporary camps, as described by the writer Hyginus, this generous suite of rooms is taken to be the centurion's quarters, although there is no explicit evidence for this. The common soldiers must have occupied the double row of rooms, which constitutes the remainder of each barrack block. Logic suggests that each pair of rooms would have accommodated a *contubernium* of eight men, but a century at full strength would then require ten pairs of rooms. In practice, the number of rooms varies from fortress to fortress. The barracks at Nijmegen have only eight pairs of rooms, but each block ends in a large room of unknown purpose. Whether these were storerooms, office space, or more luxurious accommodation for the under-officers of the century remains unknown.

Several pairs of ovens were discovered at Caerleon, set into the back of the rampart. They were perhaps allocated one per *centuria*. The excavated remains suggested that each oven comprised a domed superstructure of tiles sitting on a slabbed floor. (© Author)

Also, unlike the tribunes, for example, the centurions had no staff requiring office space; as we have seen, their subordinates, the centurial *principales*, were evidently accommodated elsewhere in the barrack block.

The centurion normally had his own latrine, at the far end of the block, where the waste outlet drained into the sewers beneath the *via sagularis*. Typical centurions' quarters were floored in the same clay and concrete already encountered in the *contubernia*, although more exotic tiled or mosaic floors have been claimed on slender evidence from Vindonissa and Bonn. All internal walls within the barrack building were plastered, and evidence of painted decoration has come from the centurions' quarters at several fortresses, including Nijmegen, Carnuntum and Caerleon. For illumination, it is likely that windows were inserted into the outer walls, and it has been suggested that, in many centurions' quarters, an area along the middle of the back wall was left unroofed, as an open courtyard. The positive benefit of bringing light and fresh air into the house may, however, have been offset by the cold, wet climate on the northern frontiers. Without the courtyard, the rearward rooms would have suffered from the same poor lighting as the men's *papiliones*.

The problem of the first cohort

Hyginus writes that 'the first cohort, since it has double strength, gets a double space allocation' (*De munit. castr.* 21). By and large, wherever the barracks of the first cohort have been identified archaeologically, they certainly occupy more space than the other cohorts, but never twice as much. From inscriptional evidence (e.g. ILS 2446), it is clear that the first cohort only ever had five centurions, the so-called *primi ordines* ('first ranks'), and it is often assumed that they must have commanded five double-strength *centuriae*.

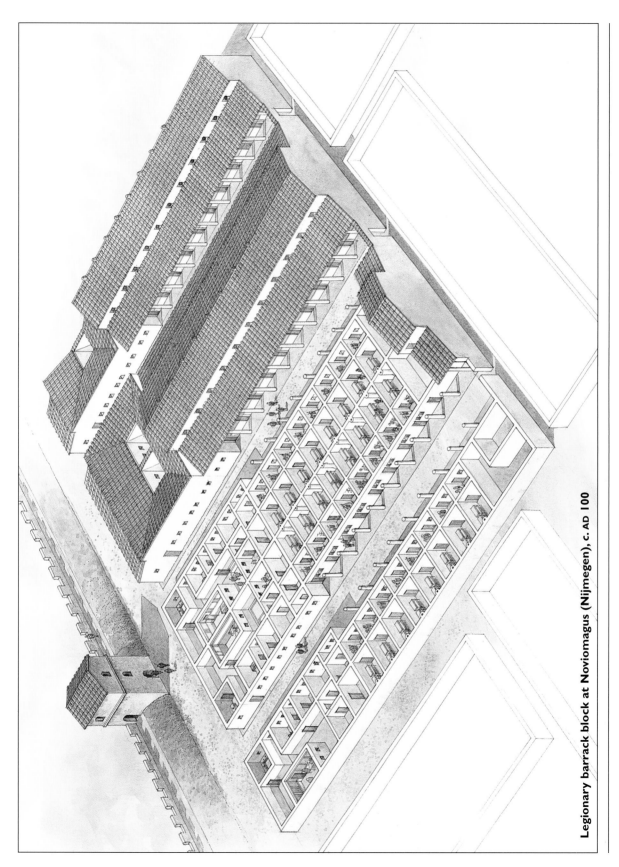

Legionary barrack block at Noviomagus (Nijmegen), c. AD 100

55

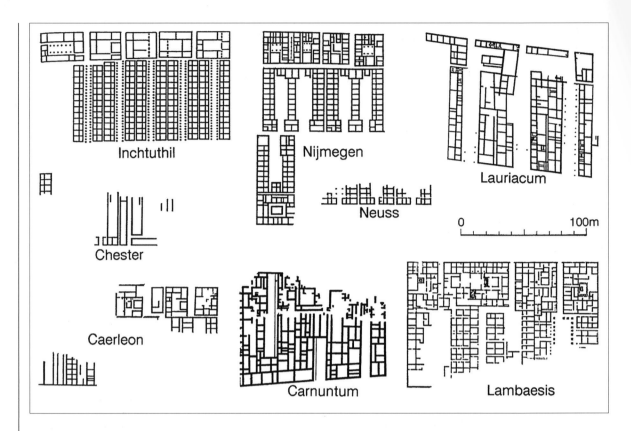

Inchtuthil

Nijmegen

Lauriacum

Chester

Neuss

0   100m

Caerleon

Carnuntum

Lambaesis

Barrack accommodation of the
first cohort in the fortresses of
Inchtuthil, Nijmegen, Lauriacum,
Chester, Neuss, Caerleon,
Carnuntum and Lambaesis. The
floor area is uniformly larger than
that provided for the other cohorts.
(© Dietwulf Baatz)

However, archaeological corroboration of this theory comes from only one site, the fortress of Inchtuthil, occupied for a few years *c.* AD 85. Here, lying to the right of the *principia*, the excavator found evidence of ten barrack blocks associated with five courtyard-type houses; these have been interpreted as the accommodation for five double centuries and five senior centurions.

Unfortunately, although several legionary fortresses can be shown to possess a similarly enlarged area to the right of the *principia*, this has rarely been investigated. At Caerleon, excavation in this area was limited; three courtyard-type houses were found, with space for another two, but the excavator's belief that there had been ten barrack blocks was never tested archaeologically. Similarly, at Lambaesis, five courtyard-type houses can be discerned with the eye of faith, but the remains of the associated barracks belong to various different building periods, making their interpretation difficult; some have claimed that only six barracks ever existed here. At Chester and Neuss the evidence is even more fragmentary owing to the size of the excavated area, and at Lauriacum the jumbled remains defy sensible interpretation. Ironically, the clearest evidence comes from the small fortress at Nijmegen, where the first cohort appears to have been located not to the right of the *principia*, but across the road in the right *praetentura*. Here, in the north-east quadrant of the fortress, were found five courtyard-type houses associated with six barrack blocks and two strip buildings, which would suggest a cohort of the normal size, with sheds for extra equipment. However, there has been a suggestion that, during the reign of Nero, there were ten barracks here as at Inchtuthil, and that the first cohort, perhaps enlarged by Vespasian, was reduced in size again by Domitian.

Aftermath: the legionary fortresses in the later period

By the end of the 2nd century AD, there were 33 legions, a marginal increase in the total originally set by Augustus. There is some evidence to suggest that a further six legions came into existence during the crisis of the 3rd century AD: Severus Alexander (AD 222–35) recruited *IV Italica*, continuing the sequence of previous emperors' *legiones Italicae*; Aurelian (AD 270–75) is thought to have raised *IV Martia*, so numbered as a companion to *III Cyrenaica* in Arabia and *I Illyricorum* as a new garrison for Phoenice; and Probus (AD 276–82), who was active in Isauria (the mountainous area of the Turkish coast opposite Cyprus), was probably responsible for legions *I*, *II* and *III Isaurae*. Finally, after the thoroughgoing reforms of the emperor Diocletian (AD 284–305), over 50 legions are thought to have been in service.

Diocletian was the great divider. Having established the Tetrarchy (or 'rule by four men') by creating joint emperors, each assisted by a junior colleague, or *Caesar*, he went on to subdivide the frontier provinces, assigning a pair of legions to each one. Thus, for example, *III Diocletiana* was raised as a sister-legion to *II Traiana* in Egypt, while the new province of Thebais on the upper Nile required two fresh units, *I Maximiana* (named after Diocletian's colleague, Maximian) and *II Flavia Constantia* (named after Maximian's *Caesar*, Flavius Constantius). Similarly, *I Noricorum* was raised in Noricum to make a pair with *II Italica*; the latter's headquarters still lay at Lauriacum, but both legions were now (or shortly afterwards) dispersed along the frontier in several smaller fortifications.

The so-called Multangular Tower at York (England) was erected in c. AD 300 at the west corner of the fortress of Eburacum. To the south-west, the river Ouse flows past the front of the fortress, and the special architecture of the tower was perhaps intended to impress visitors arriving on the waterfront. (© M. C. Bishop)

ABOVE At El-Lejjun, the main gate (*porta praetoria*) and the north gate (*porta principalis sinistra*, pictured here) were tripartite, with a central carriageway (3.5m wide) flanked by smaller side entrances (c.1.5m wide). (© Gregory Linton/Karak Resources Project)

RIGHT The four corner towers at El-Lejjun projected from the curtain wall in a wide semicircle. Excavations at the north-west corner (pictured here) revealed three rooms at ground level, and a square spiral staircase. (© Gregory Linton/Karak Resources Project)

This subdivision reached its culmination in the military reforms of Constantine (AD 306–37), who is usually credited with remodelling the legions as smaller strike forces and dispersing most of them along the frontiers. In fact, some legions had perhaps been diminishing in strength for some time. A well-known papyrus (P. Beatty Panop. 2) has allowed scholars to calculate the strengths of the two legions of western Egypt *c.* AD 300; each comprised a little more than 1,000 men. At the same time, individual legions are found divided between several locations, which implies that the parent must, at one time, have been at full strength. This, of course, is simply the logical extension of the vexillation system, whereby detachments served independently of their parent legion. The difference under Constantine is that such detachments found themselves permanently outposted. For example, in AD 294, vexillations of several Danubian legions, including *V Macedonica*, arrived in Egypt with Galerius, Diocletian's *Caesar*; a century later, around 400 soldiers stationed in

The late Roman fortress at Betthorus (El-Lejjun), c. AD 378

The ruins of this small fortress, investigated in the early years of the 20th century, were extensively excavated in the 1980s. However, the wholesale removal of stone over the centuries means that the layout of certain areas remains uncertain. The massive ramparts, around 2.5m thick, can still be seen, along with the 24 interval and corner towers, and visitors can still pick out individual buildings inside.

At only 4.7ha, the fortress covers a fraction of the area of its early imperial predecessors, but the layout is remarkably similar. The *principia* still stands at the crossroads, and barrack blocks fill the *praetentura*, but the function of the empty north quadrant is unclear and the tiny bathhouse seems inadequate for a garrison that perhaps numbered 1,000 men.

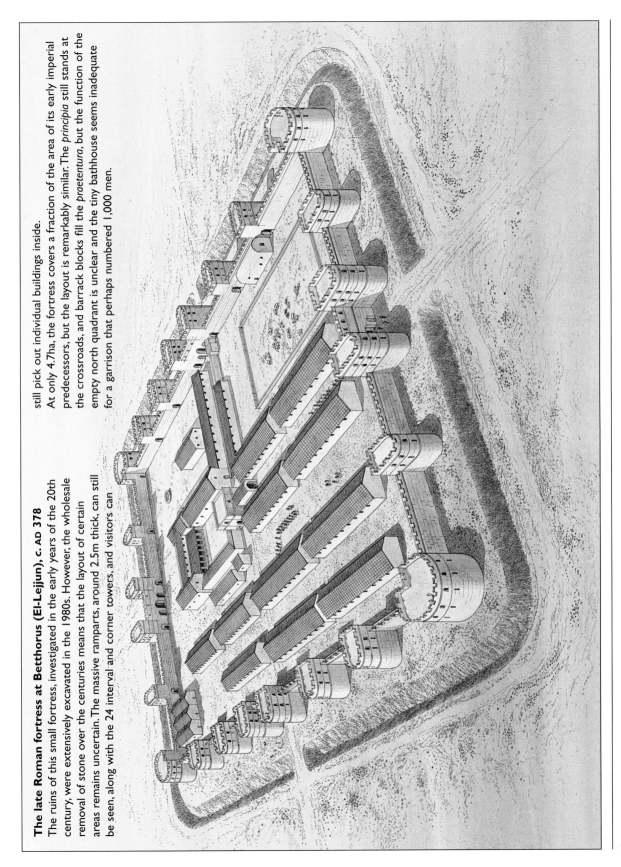

The *via principalis* at El-Lejjun (Jordan). Excavation in the 1980s clarified the jumble of building stones into a remarkably clear fortress plan. (© Gregory Linton/Karak Resources Project)

The late fortress at Udruh (Jordan) has 20 interval towers, projecting *c.*10m from the curtain wall. (© M. C. Bishop)

the Nile Delta at Memphis still described themselves as legion *V Macedonica*. Meanwhile, in Dacia Ripensis, five cohorts of the parent legion were building an imperial palace at Romuliana (Gamzigrad, Serbia), at a time when the *praefectus legionis* (all legionary commanders were by now equestrian prefects) was still based at Oescus.

Constantine fundamentally changed the Roman army by introducing a new distinction between frontier units and mobile units. In Noricum, at the end of the 4th century AD, *II Italica* was stationed at three different frontier sites including the fortress at Lauriacum, while the field army operating in Africa contained a unit of *secundani Italiciani* ('second Italicans'); thus, the original legion had been divided into four fragments, only one of which was a field unit. Its companion, *I Noricorum*, was divided between only two frontier sites, and had perhaps diminished in size during the 100 years since it was raised. Certainly, it is likely that the many legions raised by Constantine and his successors had a reduced complement. For example, the historian Ammianus Marcellinus, who served on the staff of Constantine's son Constantius II, records that, in AD 359, the 20,000 individuals besieged at Amida (Diyarbakir, Turkey) included the men of seven legions. This, and other evidence, has led

At Udruh (Jordan), the massive walls, c.3m thick, consist of a rubble core faced with limestone blocks, and still stand to a height of 6m in some places. (© M. C. Bishop)

many scholars to believe that the legions of the late empire numbered only about 1,000 men.

The few known late fortresses bear this theory out. Best known, perhaps, is the site of El-Lejjun (Jordan), which is thought to be ancient Betthorus, home of *IV Martia*. Unlike most fortresses in the west, El-Lejjun was never built over, so the Roman remains are substantially intact; the site is much denuded, however, from having been used as a quarry of reusable building stone by neighbouring peoples. Most striking is the small size of the fortress, at only 4.6ha. Excavations in the 1980s revealed that the *praetentura* initially contained 16 barrack blocks, each comprising two rows of eight rooms; there would have been room for another six blocks in the *retentura*, but no evidence of these was found. A garrison of *c*.1,000 men would not seem unreasonable. Mysteries remain, however. A splendid example of a *principia* lies at the junction of the *via praetoria* and *via principalis*, but there is no sign of a hospital or workshop; and although a large building in the right *retentura* appears to be a store building or granary, the left *retentura* seems to have been entirely vacant.

Further south in the new province of Palaestina, a strikingly similar fortress stood at Udruh (Jordan). Little is known of the interior, but the massive, towered walls enclosed an area of 4.7ha, almost identical to El-Lejjun. This suggests that it, too, was a legionary fortress, although the garrison remains unknown. By contrast, Ammianus Marcellinus records the garrison of Singara (Balad Sinjar, Iraq) in AD 360; *I Parthica* and *I Flavia* were both based there, presumably in the known 17ha fortified enclosure. Meanwhile, on the Danube, a late fortress was constructed at Troesmis for *II Herculia*; its defences enclosed only 2.8ha. Noviodunum, the base of its sister legion, *I Jovia*, was twice as large, at 5.6ha. The small size of these sites remains problematic, for other legionary fortresses appear to have continued at their original size. At Chester, for example, many of the buildings were refurbished *c.* AD 300 and were still standing 50 years later, although the special circumstances in Britain saw the garrison gradually diminish by the end of the century. The Roman legions were, by now, quite different from those of Augustus, Trajan and Marcus Aurelius, so it is unsurprising that their fortresses had also changed.

Further reading

There is no single book describing a typical legionary fortress. George Boon's work on Caerleon comes closest, while Harald von Petrikovits' study of the internal buildings from a range of fortresses has never been superseded. Many of the classic excavations were carried out at the beginning of the last century, and their publications are not always easily accessible nowadays; for example, Koenen's important excavations at Neuss appeared in the *Bonner Jahrbücher*, Vol. 111/112 (1904). However, excavations continue at many sites from year to year, and are published in local journals; for example, work at Windisch is reported in the *Jahresbericht Gesellschaft Pro Vindonissa*.

On the individual legions, Emil Ritterling's extensive entry ('Legio') in the German-language *Real-encyclopädie* is still the essential starting point, and there is much of value in Parker's *Roman Legions*, although both are now inevitably outdated. The publication of a conference held in Lyon, edited by Yann Le Bohec and Catherine Wolff, provides more recent information on many of the legions, although several of the papers are extremely abbreviated and legion *XVI Gallica* is entirely excluded. On the daily routine of the Roman soldier, the work of Roy Davies is unsurpassed; several of his more important papers have been gathered together in a volume edited by David Breeze and Valerie Maxfield.

Select bibliography

Boon, G. C., *Isca: The Roman Legionary Fortress at Caerleon, Mon.*, Cardiff: National Museum of Wales, 1972

Brewer, R. J. (ed.), *Roman Fortresses and their Legions*, Cardiff: National Museums & Galleries of Wales, 2000

Cagnat, R., *Les deux camps de la légion IIIe Auguste à Lambèse d'après les fouilles récentes*, Paris: Imprimerie Nationale, 1908

Davies, R. W., *Service in the Roman Army*, Edinburgh: Edinburgh University Press, 1989

Dyczek, C. (ed.), *Novae: 40 Lat Wykopalisk*, Warsaw: Ośrodek Badań Archeologicznych Novae, 2001

Hoffmann, B., 'The Quarters of Legionary Centurions of the Principate', *Britannia* 26, 1995, 107–51

Kennedy, D. L., *The Roman Army in Jordan*, London: Council for British Research in the Levant, 2000

Kühlborn, J.-S., *Germaniam Pacavi: Germanien habe ich befriedet*, Münster: Westfälisches Museum für Archäologie, 1995

Le Bohec, Y., and Wolff, C. (eds.), *Les légions de Rome sous le Haut-Empire*, Paris: Boccard, 2000

Parker, H. M. D., *The Roman Legions*, Oxford: Clarendon Press, 1928; repr. Chicago: Ares Publishers, 1980

Petrikovits, H. von, *Die Innenbauten römischer Legionslager während der Prinzipatszeit*, Opladen: Westdeutscher Verlag, 1975

Pitts, L. F., and St Joseph, J. K., *Inchtuthil. The Roman legionary fortress. Excavations 1952–65*, London: Society for the Promotion of Roman Studies, 1985

Ritterling, E., 'Legio', *Paulys Real-encyclopädie der classischen Altertumswissenschaft* Vol. 12, Stuttgart: Metzler, 1925

Sanader, M., *Tilurium I. Forschungen 1997–2001*, Zagreb: Golden Marketing, 2003

Zienkiewicz, J. D., *The Legionary Fortress Baths at Caerleon, Vol. 1. The Buildings*, Cardiff: National Museum of Wales, 1986

Glossary

Aedes (principiorum) shrine and repository of the legionary standards, situated centrally at the rear of the *principia*

Armamentarium armoury or weapons store (pl. *armamentaria*), several of which are arranged around the courtyard of the *principia* in many fortresses

Basilica (principiorum) colonnaded hall comprising central nave and side aisles, situated across the width of the *principia* between the courtyard and the rear suite of rooms

Basilica (thermarum) colonnaded hall, situated in the baths complex to provide a covered exercise space

Centuria unit of 80 legionaries (pl. *centuriae*), or the single barrack block which they occupy

Contubernium tent-party of eight legionaries (pl. *contubernia*), thought to occupy a single barrack room

Domus house (pl. *domūs*), specifically applied to the dwellings of the officers

Fabrica manufacturing workshop (pl. *fabricae*)

Groma surveying instrument for sighting right angles using an arrangement of four plumb lines; the point at the junction of the *via principalis* and the *via praetoria*, being the main survey point in the fortress, was also known as the *groma*

Hiberna winter quarters, sometimes within an existing township though usually a purpose-built camp, increasingly implying some degree of permanence

Horreum granary building (pl. *horrea*), designed to store grain and other foodstuffs

Intervallum space between the rampart and the buildings in the fortress

Latera praetorii the central range of buildings within the fortress (lit. 'flanks of the *praetorium*'; sing. *latus praetorii*), sandwiched between the *via principalis* and the *via quintana*

Officium office (pl. *officia*), several of which were arranged along the rear of the *principia*; also, the staff based there

Porta decumana rear gate of the fortress

Porta praetoria front gate of the fortress

Porta principalis side gate of the fortress (pl. *portae principales*), designated *sinistra* (left) or *dextra* (right) depending upon its position relative to the *principia*

Praefectus castrorum third in command of a legion, after the legate and the senior tribune

Praetentura the forward area within the fortress, extending from the front gate (*porta praetoria*) to the main lateral roadway (*via principalis*), and often filled with barrack blocks

Praetorium originally the commander's tent, later applied to his residence in the fortress

Principia the headquarters building, centrally located in the fortress and incorporating administrative offices, *armamentaria* and the *aedes*

Retentura the rear area within the fortress, extending from the rear gate (*porta decumana*) up to the secondary lateral roadway (*via quintana*), and normally filled with barrack blocks

Scamnum a block within the fortress, running parallel to the *via principalis* and containing, e.g., tribunes' houses (*scamnum tribunorum*)

Schola meeting room (pl. *scholae*) located in the *principia*, thought to have been used by the various guilds (*collegia*) of officers

Thermae the baths complex, usually incorporating an open-air exercise yard (*palaestra*), sometimes with swimming pool (*natatio*)

Tribunal raised platform (pl. *tribunalia*) for a commanding officer to address the troops

Valetudinarium hospital

Via decumana secondary longitudinal roadway in the fortress, running from the rear gate (*porta decumana*) through the *retentura*, up to the *via quintana*

Via praetoria main longitudinal roadway in the fortress, running from the front gate (*porta praetoria*) through the *praetentura*, up to the door of the *principia*

Via principalis main lateral roadway through a fortress, running across the front of the *principia* and linking the two *portae principales*

Via quintana secondary lateral roadway, separating the *retentura* from the *latera praetorii*

Via sagularis perimeter roadway, running around the *intervallum*

Index